How to Make
Wines and Cordials

ANDRÉ L. SIMON

How to Make Wines and Cordials

ANDRÉ L. SIMON

DOVER PUBLICATIONS, INC.

NEW YORK

This Dover edition, first published in 1972, is an
unabridged and unaltered republication of the work
originally published by Gramol Publications, Ltd.
in 1946 under the title *English Wines and Cordials*.

International Standard Book Number: 0-486-22860-6

Manufactured in the United States of America
Dover Publications, Inc.
180 Varick Street
New York, N. Y. 10014

CONTENTS

FOREWORD

Wine, the fermented juice of freshly gathered grapes; mead, the honey drink; ale, the barley "wine"; cider and perry, the "long" drinks fermented from apples and pears—such were the most popular beverages in England during many centuries until challenged by spirits and tea. Besides these, however, from a very early date and up to the present day, to a relatively small yet not unimportant degree, all manner of English wines and cordials have been made from fruits, flowers and seeds.

Some of these wines were intended originally as inexpensive substitutes for real wine, when real wine was taxed out of the reach of the people; they were made in the home, for home consumption, and not for sale, from elderberries, cowslips and the like of these, which were not bought, but gathered from hedges or the nearest woods. There were also English wines, older in date and of much more elaborate preparation, as well as more costly, which were really medicinal wines made from home-grown plants and imported spices. To these, various strange ingredients were often added which were intended to prevent or cure all sorts of ills and disorders. To judge from some of the prescriptions of such wines and cordials, they must have been far from pleasant to drink, but it was immaterial, since it is the effect and not the taste of a medicine which matters. There were yet other English wines and cordials, in the making of which the housewife in most homes and the still-room maid in the great houses of the country, studied both taste and effect; some were appetite-provoking, bitter "wines," and others fat-splitting or digestive cordials or, as they were sometimes called, "surfeit waters."

There was a time when practically every kind of plant and herb which grew wild in fields, copses or lanes, was credited with possessing specific medicinal properties which all country folk and many city dwellers knew of and believed in. Modern science has confirmed that their faith rested on a sound foundation in some cases, whilst in others, either the plants have lost virtues which once upon a time were theirs, or it may be that they never deserved the credit which they once enjoyed.

3

The making of English wines and cordials was entirely a home affair up to the eighteenth century, when the ever-rising cost of imported real wines was responsible for a far greater demand for home-made wines, the making of which then became a profitable commercial proposition. It was then that the practice originated of offering home-made wines under the names of imported real wines, chiefly claret, which was made in a number of different ways, either from cider, flavoured and coloured, or from raisins, black cherries, currants, etc.; champagne, made from gooseberries or currants; and port, made wholly or partly from elderberries. Other English wines, made variously, were offered under the names of Cyprus, Frontignac, Madeira, Malaga, Malta, Mountain, Rhenish, Sack and Sherry.

During the early part of the twentieth century a new technique was introduced and has since been perfected, for the making of British wines from imported raisins and grape juice, which provide the sugar matter that fermentation will transform into alcohol; the Thames or a Water Board supplies the required water for bulk, whilst essences for flavour and dyes for colour are scientifically provided. Such "wines" cannot be made at home, as the old-fashioned English wines used to be made and can still be made; they are manufactured industrially and sold commercially in very considerable quantities, but they are altogether outside the scope of the present little book, which merely purports to give a list of the old-fashioned English wines, mostly made at home and for home consumption. By way of Preface, however, we have also collected some data relating to the wines which were made from grapes in England long ago, as well as others relating to mead, ale, cider and perry, English home-made beverages all.

It would be difficult—and occasionally inadvisable—to follow all these old recipes exactly, but they will stimulate the imagination, and may well inspire present-day readers to experiment in wine-making.

4

BIBLIOGRAPHY

1669 The Closet of the eminently learned Sir Kenelme Digby Kt. opened: Whereby is discovered several ways of making Metheglin, Sider, Cherry-Wine . . . London.

1672 The Queen-like Closet or Rich Cabinet: stored with all manner of rare Receipts . . . by Hannah Wolley. London.

1691 The Britannian Magazine: or a new Art of making above twenty sorts of English Wines . . . by W.Y. London.

1706 The Way to get Wealth, or a new and easie way to make twenty-three sorts of Wine, equal to that of France . . . by Thomas Tryon. London.

1734 The practical Distiller . . . to which is added a Treatise of making artificial wines from several Fruits of the British Production . . . by G. Smith. London.

1762 The London Cook, or the whole art of cookery made easy and familiar . . . by William Gelleroy. London.

1782 The British Jewel, or Complete Housewife's best Companion . . . London.

1807 The Family Director or Housekeeper's Assistant . . . by Addison Ashburn. Coventry.

1811 The Housekeeper's and Butler's Guide, or a Directory for making and managing British Wines . . . by J. Davies. Leeds.

1814 A new system of Domestic Cookery . . . by a Lady. London.

1823 The Economist, or new Family Cookery . . . by Anthony Haselinore. London.

1830 The New London Cookery and Complete Domestic Guide . . . by a Lady. London.

1840 The female instruction or Young Woman's Companion . . . Liverpool.

1849 Indian Domestic Economy and Receipt Book . . . Bombay.

1854 Modern Cookery in all its branches . . . by Eliza Acton. 11th edition. London.

1860 The Wife's own book of Cookery . . . by Frederick Bishop. London.

1861 The Book of Household Management . . . by Mrs. Isabella Beeton. London.

1937 Herbal Delights . . . by Mrs. C. F. Leyel. Faber.

Obsolete terms occurring in some of the old recipes are explained in the books in which such recipes appear.

5

ENGLISH VINEYARDS AND WINES

WINE IS the suitably fermented juice of freshly gathered ripe grapes. There is no such thing as unfermented wine : the sweet juice of the grape does not begin to be wine until it begins to ferment. Fermentation is a perfectly natural process, by which a very unstable form of "carbohydrate," the sugars present in the juice of ripe grapes, readjusts its molecules of carbon, hydrogen and oxygen in such a way that, in the end, there is no trace of the original grape sugar left, but, in its place, there is a different and more stable form of "carbohydrate," called ethyl alcohol, which is a source of heat, like the sugar from which it came, but in a more immediately available form. All wines contain more or less alcohol, rather less than more, and always a great deal more water than anything else. Wines known as "beverage" or "natural" or "light" wines may contain as much as $14\frac{1}{2}\%$ of alcohol, but the majority of them contain rather less than 10%. Wines known as "fortified" contain on an average twice as much alcohol as the others.

Although there is bound to be some alcohol in all wines, the importance of alcohol in wine is somewhat like the importance of canvas, board, paper or whatever material the artist must have before he can begin to paint a picture : but we do not buy a picture because of the quality, texture or weight of the canvas or board upon which it is painted : what we look at, appraise and appreciate is the picture itself, the work of the artist. So it is with wine. The background of ethyl alcohol merely serves to bring out and hold together the pleasing colour, attractive

6

fragrance and delicious taste of the wine itself: these are the real picture, the work of the artist, both a physical and intellectual joy for the connoisseur, that is, he or she who is blessed with a keen and trained sense of appreciation. Alcohol has neither colour, smell, nor taste of its own, but it holds in the right perspective and shows off the colour, "bouquet" and flavour of the wine.

One might as well try to count the pebbles of the beach as the wines of the world; although they all have in common a large proportion of water and a small proportion of alcohol, they are all different. Wines vary not only from country to country, from vineyard to vineyard and from year to year, but from bottle to bottle. The species of grapes from which the wine is made; the nature of the soil of the vineyards; the number of hours of sunshine and of inches of rain in any one year, and their incidence; the skill or lack of skill of individual *vignerons* at all times, but more particularly at the all-important time of the vintage; the manner and degree of the pressing of the freshly gathered grapes and the rate at which fermentation proceeds; these and a number of other factors are responsible for the differences which exist in the quality, appearance and individuality of the immense tide of wine which surges forth, year after year, from the vineyards of the world. Besides which, we must never forget that wine, like man, has its life to live, being, at first, too young and too green to be good company, then growing to full manhood, always liable, however, to lapses and sickness, from which it recovers provided proper care be given in time : it is then a true friend and companion. Eventually it gets feeble, sick, sour, and then it dies. And whether the life of any wine be short or long depends very much upon the keeper in the neck of its bottle-home—the cork— which should allow just a very little oxygen to filter through, so that the wine within may breathe. When the cork fails, when it lets mould or weevils get hold of it, the wine within that bottle is doomed.

Wine, of course, has a much wider meaning, when qualified and used in conjunction with other words. Shakespeare speaks of the "wine of life," and when brewers are in a poetical mood they refer to beer as "barley wine." There are also the elderberry, rhubarb, cowslip, ginger "wines" and many such fruit, flower, herb or sap wines, wines in the sense that they are

7

alcoholic beverages, and that their alcohol backbone is due to fermentation, but their flavour is that of the materials from which they are made, and the names of these being clearly stated, nobody expects freshly gathered grapes to have anything to do with their confection.

English wines and *British wines* are not such precise denominations, but the fact that grapes are not grown commercially in England for the purpose of wine-making is so well known that nobody expects a bottle of English or British wine to contain real wine—that is, the fermented juice of freshly gathered ripe grapes—but some sort of fruit or artificial wine of rather higher alcoholic strength than the average "natural" wine. It is so now, but it was not ever thus. There was a time, a long while ago, when English wine, like French or Italian or any other wine, was the wine that was made in England from freshly gathered ripe grapes from English vineyards.

There is no documentary evidence that the Romans, during their occupation of Britain, attempted to plant vineyards and to show the natives how to make wine. But there is ample evidence that the early Christian Church did introduce viticulture in these islands, and that grapes were grown, for the purpose of making wine, in many parts of England, as well as in Wales and as far north as Scotland.

However, we cannot accept as a fact Dr. Plott's statement that "the Britons planted vineyards and made wines anciently over all the kingdom." There is no documentary evidence whatever to warrant such an assertion, whereas we have the trustworthy testimony of the Venerable Bede (672–735) who tells us that, at the beginning of the eighth century, at the time when he was writing, the culture of the vine had made *some* progress in Britain, and that there were vineyards in *a few* places—"*vineas quibiscum in locis germinans.*"

The culture of the vine in England, at any time and under whatever conditions, cannot have been attended with sufficient success to have induced the Britons to have vineyards "over all the kingdom." Besides the religious Houses, for whom viticulture was a necessity, the King and a few wealthy landowners had vineyards, for pleasure more than for profit. These were situated in widely scattered parts of the land, and whilst they were comparatively numerous, they must have been mostly very small, to judge from the extremely low cost of their upkeep.

8

In the laws of Alfred (871–901) there is mention of a vineyard, and Edgar (957–975) made a gift of a vineyard, situated at Wycet, together with the vine-dressers on the estate.

After the Norman Conquest, the number of English vineyards increased rapidly, but they were cultivated, according to Camden, to no mercantile purpose; the home-made wines of the Norman kings and lords were drunk at their table only, and it cannot be said that viticulture in England bears any direct relation to the English wine trade.

It is a subject, however, which possesses sufficient features of interest in connection with the history of English wines or the wines made in England, to be dealt with here at some length.

The culture of the vine received renewed, and probably more scientific, attention after the Conquest. In many districts, especially where great religious establishments existed, vineyards were to be seen : Worcester, Gloucester, Tewkesbury, Hereford and Ledbury can still point to the ancient sites of their former vineyards. There are also proofs that vineyards were planted, among other places, in the village of Westminster; at Chenetone, in Middlesex; at Ware, in Hertfordshire; at Hanten, in Worcestershire, and at Winchester.

In Domesday Book, under the title of *Rageneia*, there is a record of six arpents of vines, among the lands of Suein, in Essex, which, it is said, yielded twenty casks (*modii*) of wine in good years. Henry de Ferrieres is also mentioned in Domesday as the owner of twelve arpents planted in vines at Bisham, in Berkshire.

Vines were even grown at the Abbey of Ramsey, in East Anglia, although this monastery was situated in the midst of a watery fen, accessible only on one side by an artificial causeway, and surrounded by ash and alder woods. In the chronicles of the abbey, vine-dressers, *vinitores*, are mentioned as forming part of the lay staff of labourers, during the reign of Henry I, in 1114 and 1134.

In the register of Spalding Priory, we read of John, the Almoner, who bought lands, laid out a garden, and planted a vineyard and orchards—*plantavit vineam et pomeria*.

Towards the middle of the twelfth century, so we are told by William of Malmesbury, vineyards were no longer confined to a few places, but extended over large tracts of country, producing a great quantity of excellent wine : "You may behold," he observes, when describing the fertility of the vale at Gloucester, "the paths and public roads fenced with apple trees, which are not planted by the hand of man but grow spontaneously. . . .

"This district, too, exhibits a greater number of vineyards than any other county in England, yielding abundant crops and of superior quality; nor are the wines made here by any means harsh or ungrateful to the palate, for, in point of sweetness, they may almost bear comparison with the growths of France."

In the reign of Stephen there is a mention, in 1140, of two vineyards at Maldon, and, in the same year, the Sheriffs of Northamptonshire and Leicestershire were allowed, in their accounts, "for the livery of the King's vine-dresser at Rockingham, and for necessaries for the vineyards." There is also an Act of this monarch, which is undated, but which from internal evidence may be safely attributed to A.D. 1143, ordering that restoration should be made to Holy Trinity Priory, London, of its land in Smithfield, which Geoffrey, Earl of Essex, had seized and converted into a vineyard.

Among the appendages to the Castle of Windsor at this period was the vineyard. The pay of the vintager and the expense of gathering the grapes are among the regular annual charges relating to Windsor on the Pipe Rolls, from the commencement of the series in 1155. Lambarde says that in the Records "it moreover appearethe that tythe hathe bene payed of wyne pressed out of grapes that grewe in the Little Parke theare, to the abbot of Waltham, which was parson bothe of the Old and New Wyndsore, and that accompts have bene made of the charges of planting the vines that grewe in the saide parke, as also of making the wynes, whearof somme partes weare spent in the householde, and somme solde for the kinges profyt".[1]

Stow gives a similar account. He says that in the Records of the Honour Court of Windsor Castle, held in the outer Gate-House, "is to be seene the yeerely account of the charges of the planting of the vines that in the time of K. Richard the Second grew in great plenty within ye Litle Parke, as also of the making of the wine it selfe".[2] Richard III, in the first year of his reign,

[1] "Dictionarium Angliæ Topographicum et Historicum." The Hon. Daines Barrington doubted the correctness of Lambarde, as he did not give his authority for the statement. (Archæologia, vol. III, p. 176.) Recent researches, however, prove Lambarde's accuracy.

[2] "Annales," by Howes, p. 143, edit. 1631, See Dissertations, by

granted to John Piers the "Office of Master of our Vyneyarde of Vynes nigh unto our Castell of Wyndesore, and otherwise called the office of Keeper of our Gardyne called the Vyneyarde nigh unto our said Castell, to have and occupie the same office, by him or his deputie sufficient, for terme of his lyff, with the wages and fees of vi.d. by the day".[3]

In the fourth year of the reign of Henry II, payments appear to have been made and charged to the Royal Exchequer for the keeper of the vineyard, who received on one occasion sixty shillings and tenpence, as well as for the expenses of the said royal vineyard. Later on, during the same reign, in 1159, 1162, 1165, 1174 and 1175, there are frequent mentions of the royal vineyards at Windsor, Purley, Stoke, Cistelet, and in Herefordshire and Huntingdonshire; in 1165 there is an entry of a vineyard at Tenham, the produce of which seems to have been devoted to the sick at the infirmary.

During the first year of the reign of King Richard there are three mentions of vineyards, and others occur during the reign of Henry III, at Lincoln, Bath and Hereford; during the reign of Edward II at York; and as late as the reign of Richard II, in 1385 and 1392, at Windsor and Kennington. At the beginning of Edward I's reign, in 1276, Cantilupe, Bishop of Hereford, either planted or renewed the vineyard which his pupil and successor, Swinfield, had at Ledbury. In 1289, the Bishop made seven casks (*dolia*) of white wine and nearly one of verjuice at Ledbury. This wine was chiefly transferred to Bosbury, another estate of the Bishop, and it was mostly drunk during the ensuing summer.

Ledbury must have been particularly well suited for the culture of the grape vine, since as late as the end of the seventeenth century, George Skipp, a descendant of Bishop Skipp, made both red and white wine from his plantation at Upper Hall, in the parish of Ledbury.

According to Somner, Canterbury Church and St. Augustine's Abbey were possessed of numerous vineyards, amongst which those at Colton, St. Martin's, Chertham, Brook and Hollingbury are specially named.

At Halling, near Rochester, the Bishop of that See is stated

Samuel Pegge and Daines Barrington, on the former Cultivation of the Vine in England, "Archæologia," vol. I, p. 319, and vol. V, p. 67.

[3] MS. Harl., No. 438, f. 135.

by Lambarde to have had a vineyard and to have made wine, of which a present was sent to Edward II; according to the same authority, there used to be, after the Conquest, a great many vines at Santlac, near Battle, in Sussex, probably belonging to the abbey of that name.

Having a staff of skilled vine-dressers and many vines to which much labour and money had been devoted for some years, Churchmen were loth to give up this culture; at the same time, being able to obtain much better wines from the Continent at lower cost, they did not feel bound to drink the produce of their own vineyards, and they attempted to sell at any rate some of it.

The archives of the Church of Ely have preserved an account of such transactions, which shows how little saleable home-grown wine was made, and that the grapes often failed to ripen properly, verjuice being all that could be made :

	£	s.	d.
Exitus vineti	2	15	3½
Exitus vineæ	10	12	2½
Ten bushels of grapes from the vineyard ..		7	6
Seven dolia musti from the vineyard, 12 Edw. II	15	1	0
Wine sold for	1	12	0
Verjuice	1	7	0
One dolium and one pipe filled with new wine and supplied at Ely.			
For wine out of this vineyard	1	2	2
For verjuice from thence		16	0

No wine but verjuice made, 9 Edw. IV.

An entry in a Pipe Roll of the Bishopric of Winchester for the year 1208–9 shows that the Bishop of that See also sold wines, although it is not recorded whether they were home-grown or of foreign origin.

We are told by Stowe that, among the archives at the Court of Pleas of the Forest and Honours at Windsor : "is to be seen the yearly account of the charges of the planting of the vines, that in the time of King Richard II grew in great plenty within the little park, as also the making of the wine itself, whereof some part was spent in the King's house, and some part sold to his profit, the tithes whereof were paid to the abbot of Waltham then parson both of the New and Old Windlesore."

As regards the manner and mode employed for cultivating vineyards in England during the early Middle Ages, the only evidence we have is that furnished by William of Malmesbury who, describing the domain of Thorney, in the Isle of Ely, which he compares to an earthly Paradise, says : "It is so fully cultivated that no portion of the soil is left unoccupied. On the one hand, it may be seen thickly studded with apple trees; on the other covered with vines, which either trail along the ground, or are trained on high and supported on poles."

This last passage alone should have convinced those historians who have always denied the possibility of vines being grown and wine being made in England. Mr. Barriston, for instance, has argued that the early chroniclers meant perry or cider, and not wine, when they wrote *vinum;* such an argument is absolutely groundless, since words existed for both perry and cider, as appears in an account of 1174, when six shillings and eightpence were paid to the farmer of Windsor for *Wine and Perry and Cider—et in custamento Vini et Pirati et Siceræ, VIs. et VIIId.*

According to Twyne, the decay of the culture of the vine in England dates from the reign of Henry III, when the possession of Guyenne had been assured, and when the great influx of wines from Gascony, which characterised the reign of King John, had shown the husbandman that land could be turned to better account in England. During the next three hundred years, however, the wines which were freely imported and consumed in England mostly came from the overseas vineyards of the realm, and were entitled to the name of English wines.

THE WINES OF GASCONY AND OTHERS

IN 1152, Henri Plantagenet, Duke of Anjou and Normandy,
married the richest heiress in Christendom, Eleanor of Aquitaine.
Two years later, when he became King of England, the
whole of the already flourishing vineyards of Bordeaux became
part of the realm of England and remained under English rule
for some three hundred years. During that long spell the
men of Bordeaux and the whole of Gascony were welcomed in
England as the King's subjects : their wines, which were usually
known as *Wines of Gascony*, enjoyed a privileged status : they
were drunk by all but the poorest throughout the land. There
were no glass bottles, and no corks in those days : wine was
drunk mostly within the first twelve months after being made,
and "old wine," as wine was called which was over one year
old, usually fetched even less money than cheap "new" wine,
the inference being that this "old wine," not being properly
kept, soon became vinegar.

It was also during the reign of Edward III that the practice
originated of a number of ships, sailing from some appointed
English port, and, on some officially appointed day, proceeding
to Bordeaux in fleet formation, in order to be better able to
defend themselves from attack. Such fleets sailed usually in
the late autumn and returned home before Christmas with the
"new" wines; they sailed again in the following spring, usually
soon after Easter, and returned with the "rack" wines.

When the wine-laden ships reached an English port, the attorneys of the King's Butler, or "Yeoman of the Butlery," had to be advised; their office consisted in taking two casks of wine per ship, or their equivalent value in money, for the King's right of "prise" or "prisage"; they also purchased whatever quantity of wine they had been instructed to secure for the royal cellars and the army, as well as for the numerous lay and ecclesiastical beneficiaries of the King's bounty.

Only then could the wine be landed and stored in vaults on or near the quayside. This landing had to be effected by officially recognised "wine-drawers," skilled in this work, who enjoyed an absolute monopoly.

Once landed, the wine had to be passed by the "gauger," the buyer and seller each paying this official one halfpenny per tun of wine gauged, and it could then be sold; but, again, the services of an official "broker" were required to make the sale binding. This broker had to see that the price demanded by the seller was not beyond the "maximum" price fixed by royal authority from time to time for different sorts of wine; he also had to see that the importer of wine sold his wine wholesale, and only to those who were free to buy wholesale, viz., peers of the realm, vintners and taverners.

The retailer of wine had also to comply with many royal and municipal ordinances. The maximum retail prices of wine were fixed by law; besides this, wines of different kinds were not allowed to be kept in the same cellar, so that they could not be mixed together; the consumer had the right to see his wine drawn from the cask; the Vintners' Company in London, and municipal authorities in the provinces, had the right to enter the premises of any taverner and demand to test the wines stored therein and condemn them to be destroyed if they thought fit.

Irksome as these regulations undoubtedly were, they had all been framed with a view to giving the consumer the greatest possible protection against fakers and profiteers, a protection for which the consumer was made to pay ultimately, since the different taxes levied by all the officials through whose hands all wines had to pass were charged for in the retail price of the wine.

Prices, however, remained sufficiently low during five hundred years for wine to be within the reach of a very large number of people throughout the land.

From twelfth-century records we learn that the average price of wine in England was then $1d$. per gallon. The lowest rate at which we find wine quoted is under $\frac{1}{2}d$. per gallon, in 1159 in London; and the highest is $2d$. per gallon, in 1174, for "French" and "Moselle" wines.

During the thirteenth century, "wine," "Gascon" wine and wines of "Anjou," "Auxerre," "Oléron," "France," "La Reole" and "Moselle," were sold in all parts of the country at prices varying from $\frac{3}{4}d$. up to $3\frac{1}{2}d$. per gallon, the average price being about $2d$. per gallon. Towards the end of the century we find mention, for the first time, of "Ossey" and "Malvoisie," which were imported from further south and sold at much higher rates, viz., $6d$. and $8d$. per gallon respectively.

During the fourteenth century the average price of "Gascon" wine, the wine which then formed probably 80% of the total wine imports, rose to about $3\frac{1}{2}d$. per gallon. The lowest recorded was $2\frac{1}{4}d$., in 1343, at Berwick-on-Tweed; the highest $4\frac{1}{4}d$., in London in 1338. Poitou and Rochelle wines cost rather less than "Gascon," and there was a rate of $1\frac{1}{2}d$. per gallon charged in London, in 1303, for "old wine," which meant, perhaps, "too old," i.e., defective wine.

On the other hand, "Vernage," a sweet wine from Italy, was sold at $2s$. per gallon, at Durham, in 1335, and "Crete" wine at $4s$., in 1360. Rhine wine was sold at $1s$. $2d$. per gallon in 1340, at Durham; at $6\frac{1}{2}d$. in 1367; and $11d$. in 1380, at King's Lynn.

During the fifteenth century the price of "Gascon" wine was fixed at $6d$. per gallon, by order, but it fetched commonly $7d$. or $8d$. per gallon. The chief feature of this century is the decline in the consumption of "Gascon," or beverage wine, and the increased popularity of a large variety of sweet, or at any rate, sweeter, wines from Spain, Portugal, Italy and the islands of the Mediterranean, such were "Bastard," "Tyre," "Romeney," "Malmsey," "Oseye," "Vernage" and "Hippocras." Irrespective of the "assize" or official maximum prices of all such wines, their cost varied greatly according to their quality, style, scarcity and popularity; thus, whilst "Malmsey" cost but $10d$. per gallon at Norwich, in 1424, and "Oseye" $1s$. at Warwick, in 1405, and at Cambridge in 1414; "Vernage" cost $2s$. $8d$. per gallon at Warwick, in 1405, and "Hippocras" $3s$. $4d$., at Cambridge in 1488.

During the sixteenth century references to "Gascon" wine are much less numerous : this wine was still imported on a large scale, but was more commonly known under the name of "Claret," the price of which rose steadily from 8*d*. per gallon in 1510, to 2*s*. 8*d*. in 1592, in spite of the fact that its "assize" price was only 8*d*. per gallon in 1538 and 1539, 1*s*. in 1565, 1*s*. 1*d*. in 1571, and 1*s*. 4*d*. from 1578 to 1581. The price of Rhenish wine also rose from 1*s*. per gallon in 1508, to 3*s*. 4*d*. in 1594.

The sweet wines of all kinds, "Malmseys," "Muscadells" and "Muscadine," "Romeney," "Fimoy," "Hippocras," etc., continued to be imported largely and were sold at prices varying from 10*d*. per gallon to as much as 8*s*. (for "Hippocras"), in 1587.

The chief feature of the wine trade during the sixteenth century was the introduction and the immediate popularity of "Sack," the price of which rose from 10*d*. per gallon in 1533, to 4*s*. 8*d*. in 1598, in spite of the fact that its "assize" price was but 1*s*. 1*d*. per gallon as late as 1571.

The cheapest wines of all during the sixteenth century were those shipped to England from La Rochelle, mostly thin white wines from Poitou and Augoumois, but their price rose very much during the latter part of the century. Their "assize" price was only 4*d*. per gallon as late as 1553, but it was fixed at 1*s*. 2*d*. from 1578 to 1581.

During the fifteenth century, when Bordeaux and its vineyards returned to the allegiance of the King of France, the cost of claret in England rose, but not nearly so much as might have been expected. Even a hundred years later, in 1553, the "assize" or maximum price of claret in London was fixed at £5 per tun, or 8*d*. per gallon. Soon after, however, the price of wine rose steadily, so much so that, in 1575, the assize was fixed at £10 per tun, a rate which was evidently below the real "market" value of wine, since it is on record that £12 10*s*. per tun was the price paid, in 1575, for Gascon wine purchased for Queen Elizabeth. By the end of the century the price of Gascon wine had risen to 2*s*. 8*d*. per gallon in London, whilst sack and sweet wines cost 4*s*. per gallon.

During the seventeenth century this upward trend of wine prices was accelerated by ever-rising taxation which, at times, gave place to total prohibition, in the reigns of the last two

Stuarts and that of William III. William III raised the duties on wine, in 1693, and inaugurated the imposition of a scale of duties on different wines according to their country of origin : thus, French wine paid £22 2s 10d. per tun; Rhenish wine, £19 15s. 3d. per tun; and Spanish and Portugese wines £17 13s. 3d. per tun. The same principle was adhered to in 1697, when the duties on French, Rhenish and Peninsular wines were raised to £47 2s. 10d., £26 2s. 10d. and £21 12s. 5d. respectively.

As a consequence, more and more people in England found themselves obliged to give up drinking imported wines, and it was then that they turned their attention to the making of fermented beverages from fresh fruits, herbs and various plants which were plentiful and quite inexpensive. Fruits, of course, had to be purchased or cultivated, but some of the more popular English wines were made, and are still made, from elderberry, cowslip and weeds which cost absolutely nothing but the trouble of gathering them where they grew along the roadside, in spinneys and grasslands. Of course, none of the "herb" wines had any chance to "ferment" unless generously sweetened with cane sugar, the supply of which, as it happened, was also abundant for the first time during the seventeenth century.

ENGLISH WINES AND CORDIALS

BEFORE MAN settles anywhere, he makes sure that there is water for himself and the animals he has domesticated. This is a rule with no exception. It has been the same from the beginning of time, and in all climes. Man cannot live without water, but, if he has nothing more cheerful to drink than water, man's life is a dog's life. Hence among all nations and in all times men have not only made wine from grapes and ale from barley, but they have also pressed into their service all the fruits of the earth, figuratively and realistically, not so much to quench their normal or animal thirst, as to gratify a peculiarly human craving for something wet with a taste, a smell, and a "kick" in it.

The Egyptians of the earliest dynasties made wines from figs, dates, pomegranates and other fruits, and they also flavoured their drinks with rue, hellebore, wormwood and other highly scented plants. The Assyrians, the Hittites and the ancient Hebrews made wines from the carrob or locust bean, from the sap of palm trees and other trees, as well as from all sorts of fruits. The art of making various fruit wines was also well understood by the Romans : Pliny mentions wines made from medlars, figs, sorbs, mulberries, palms and a number of aromatic herbs.

In England, the same art reached a very high degree of perfection during the seventeenth and eighteenth centuries, owing to the fact that a great many fruits had by then been imported and were cultivated with success, and also because the moist climate of the country is highly suitable for the free growth of many berries.

Among English fruits proper, the more extensively grown and used in the making of beverages were, in the first place, apples and pears, and then cherries, followed by damsons and plums, apricots and peaches, figs and quinces. Among imported fruits which were commonly used in the making of English wines were oranges, lemons and raisins. Many of the home-made wines, however, were not made from pip or stone fruits, but from berries, such as brambles or blackberries, black currants, red and white currants, elderberries, dewberries, gooseberries, mulberries, raspberries and strawberries. There were some English wines made from such roots as turnips and parsnips, and from the sap of such trees as the birch and sycamore. Lastly, there was quite a range of home-made wines which were made from grapes or any fruit available and were flavoured with the leaves or blooms of various English weeds, grasses and flowers, such as balm, carnations, clary, cowslips, dandelion, gilliflower, marigold, primroses, roses, sage or scurvy grass. A favourite "wine," and a still more popular "beer," were also flavoured with the root of imported ginger.

The reason why English wines and cordials had not been made upon anything like the same important scale before the seventeenth century was the high cost of sugar in England up to then. Honey had been the only sweetening agent previous to the discovery of America : it was used in the making of Mead and Metheglin and to sweeten many drinks, but the quantities available were too limited for general use in the making of fruit wines. It was also some time before the cane sugar from the West Indies could be obtained in England at a price sufficiently low to justify its use for the making of wines and cordials.

Great as the number of English wines may be, the number of English cordials is far greater, since there is no limit to human imagination and inventiveness, and cordials may be made in a great many different ways, using the same ingredients in different proportions or combinations. Most of them have some form of spirit as a basis, as well as more or less sugar to sweeten them. But their colour, taste and smell vary very much. It may be said, however, that when they bear the name of some fruit, herb or spice, it is that which is responsible for their more outstanding flavour or savour.

ALLSPICE

Allspice, another name for Jamaica Pepper, is the fruit of a West Indian tree which grows to a height of 30 feet. Allspice must be gathered before it is ripe, otherwise it loses its aromatic scent : it is then dried and, if of good quality, the dried berries should contain 60% of *Phenol Eugenol*, the alkaloid responsible for their pungent scent.

Allspice is used chiefly in the making of punch, either in the ground form, or as Allspice Water, a highly aromatic water obtained by macerating bruised allspice berries for some hours in plain spirit.

ANGELICA

Angelica is an alpine plant which grows freely from Lapland to Spain. Its roots, stems and seeds all possess a musk-like scent which is both discreet and pleasing. In Lapland they dry the leaves and smoke them like tobacco; in France, angelica is cultivated on a large scale for the making of liqueurs and sweets. In England, the stalks are sometimes candied and the young shoots eaten in salads.

ANGELICA WATER

Take 8 handfuls of the leaves, wash them and cut them and lay them on a table to dry; when they are dry put them into an earthen pot and put to them 4 quarts of strong wine; let it stay for 24 hours, but stir it twice in the time; then put it into a warm still or an alembic and draw it off.

Mrs. Leyel, Herbal Delights.

ANGELICA WATER

Wash and cut some angelica leaves, and lay them to dry. When quite dry, throw them into an earthen pot, and put to them four quarts of strong wine lees. Infuse it twenty-four hours, stirring it twice in that time. Then put it into a warm still, or an alembic, and draw it off. Cover your bottles with paper, prick holes in it, and let it stand two or three days. Then mix all together, sweeten it, and when settled, bottle it, cork it close, and set it by for use.

Anthony Haselmore (1823).

ANISEED

An annual plant with bright green feathery leaves is aniseed; it is a native of the Mediterranean basin, but was introduced into England during the fourteenth century and grows well in most parts of the British Isles, although its seeds do not ripen except in exceptionally hot summers. The seeds contain an aromatic oil and they are used in the making of liqueurs and cordials.

ANNISEED WATER

Take a pound of good anniseeds, steep them by infusion in three gallons of spirits of low-wines, or proof-spirits; but if your spirits are high proof, you may add a little water in the distillation, and then draw off the quantity the spirits were. And this rule may properly be used for distilling all common waters with seeds, were it not that the quantity is diversified according as they are in strength; for of cardamums you must put two pounds to the like quantity of spirits : and as to the herbs angelica, mint, wormwood, and balm, they are properly to be gathered in their prime, and dried in the shade, that the sun, with their moisture, draw not out their virtue too powerfully; and the proportion is varied, according as you would have the water more or less in strength of the herb; and in this case you must consider the strength of the herb, and accordingly proportion them; for a handful of wormwood or cardus will go farther than three or four of balm, mint, etc.

The Way to get Wealth (1706).

ANNISEED

For four bottles of brandy, take half a pound of anniseeds, a quarter of a pound of fennel, three cloves cut in small bits, with a little salt; put all in the brandy, and infuse it twelve hours before you distil it; two pounds of sugar must be clarified, with two bottles and a half of water, and the whites of two or three eggs beaten well together.

Duncan Macdonald, New London Family Cook (c. 1800).

ANISEED

For three gallons, take seven quarts of rectified malt spirit, five pennyweights of the oil of aniseed, one pound of loaf sugar,

one gill of spirit of wine, and fill up with water. Fine this with
alum only.

J. Davies (1811).

APPLE

The fruit of any member of the genus *Malus*, of which there
are a very considerable number of species : these may be roughly
divided into four groups : 1. crab apples, the parent species
from which all others have been evolved; 2. cooking apples,
usually large and either pale green or yellow; 3. dessert apples,
usually smaller, darker of skin, sweeter of taste and more fragrant; 4. cider apples, usually smaller than the cooking apples,
but also rather light, and mostly green in colour, and very
acid. They are the best for making Cider, Apple Wine and
Apple Jack. (See CIDER.)

APPLE WINE

Add to a barrel of cider the herb scarlea, the quintessence of
wine, a little nitre, and a pound of syrup of honey. Let it
work in the cask till clear and well settled, then draw it off,
and it will be little inferior to Rhenish, either in clearness,
colour or flavour.

Bishop (1860).

APRICOT

The fruit of the apricot tree, a native of North China which
was brought to Armenia many years ago : it has since been
introduced and is now extensively cultivated in most temperate
countries. Apricots were used to make apricot wine in England,
years ago, and they are still used to make apricot brandy and
apricot liqueurs.

APRICOT BRANDY

A highly flavoured and rather fascinating liqueur compounded
in England and elsewhere; brandy is used in the making of the
better sorts; cheaper spirit for inferior brands; in all cases the
flavour is imparted by dried apricots. The best apricot brandy,
however, is distilled from fresh apricots and the crushed kernels
of their stones, in lands where apricots bear abundant fruit,
such as Hungary, where they make a very good apricot brandy;
it is sold under the label *Barat Palinka*, in quite distinctive
odd-shaped bottles.

23

APRICOT LIQUEUR

A sweetened apricot brandy of rather low alcoholic strength. Many cordial and liqueur compounders produce apricot liqueurs which differ in strength, sweetness and attractiveness, as well as price : they are mostly sold under registered and advertised brands such as *Abricotine, Apry,* etc.

TO MAKE APRICOT WINE

Take three pounds of sugar and three quarts of water, let them boil together, and skim it well; then put in six pounds of apricots pared and stoned, and let them boil till they are tender; then take them up, and when the liquor is cold bottle it up; you may if you please, after you have taken out the apricots, let the liquor have one boil with a sprig of flowered clary in it; the apricots make a marmalade, and are very good for present spending.

Gelleroy—London Cook (1762).

TO MAKE APRICOT WINE

Put to every quart of water a pound and a half of apricots which are not over ripe, let them be wiped clean, and cut in pieces; boil these till the liquor is strong of the apricot flavour, then strain the liquor through a sieve, and put to every quart four or five ounces of white sugar; boil it again and scum it, and when the scum rises no more, pour it into an earthen pot; the day following bottle it, putting into every bottle a lump of loaf sugar as big as a nutmeg; this will presently be fit for drinking, and is a very pleasant liquor, but it will not keep long.

The British Jewel (1782).

TO MAKE APRICOT WINE

To 2 gallons of spring water take 8 lb. ripe apricots. Slice them into the water, put in 5 lb. loaf sugar. Let it all boil some time, and then begin to scum it, it must be nicely scummed (you may put the scum into a clean sieve set in a pot to save what liquor comes from it). When the wine is as clear as you can make it, from the drops of sugar, pour it hot on the kernels, which must be cracked, and put with the shells into the pan you intend the liquor to cool in, stir it together and cover it. Work it with a toast and yeast, and in 2 or 3 days, when it settles, fine it into your vessel, and let it work as it will. When

24

it has done working, pour in a bottle of Rhenish or small white wine; stop it up for six months, and then if very fine, bottle it and keep it 12 months.

Eighteenth-century MS.

APRICOT WINE

Take twelve pounds of apricots when nearly ripe, wipe them clean, and cut them in pieces : then put them into two gallons of water, and let them boil till the water has strongly imbibed the flavour of the fruit : then strain the liquor through a hair sieve, and put to every quart of liquor six ounces of sugar : after which boil it again, and skim it; and when the scum has ceased to rise, pour it into an earthen vessel. Next day, bottle it, putting a lump of sugar into every bottle.

J. Davies (1811).

AQUA MIRABILIS
TO MAKE AQUA MIRABILIS (A VERY DELICATE WAY)

Take three pints of sack, three pints of white wine, one quart of the spirit of wine, one quart of the juice of celandine leaves, of melitot-flowers, cardamum-seeds, cubebs, galingale, nutmegs, cloves, mace, ginger, two drams of each; bruise them and mix them with the wine and spirits, let it stand all night in the still, not an alembeck, but a common still, close stopped with rye paste; the next morning make a slow fire in the still and all the while it is stilling, keep a wet cloth about the neck of the still, and put as much white sugar candy as you think fit into the glass where it drops.

Queen-like Closet, Hannah Wolley (1672).

AQUA MIRABILIS

Take cubebs, cardamums, galingals, nutmegs, mace, cloves and cinnamon, of each two drachms, and bruise them small. Then take a pint of the juice of calendine, half a pint each of the juices of spearmint, and of balm, flowers of melilot, cowslip, rosemary, borrage, bugloss, and marigolds, of each three drachms; seeds of fennel, coriander, and carraway, of each two drachms; two quarts of the best sack, and a quart of white wine; brandy, the strongest angelica, and rose water, of each a pint. Bruise the spices and seeds and steep them, with the herbs and flowers, in the juices, waters, sack, white wine, and brandy, all night. In the morning distil it in a common still pasted up, and from this quantity you may draw off a gallon at least. Sweeten to the taste with sugar candy, bottle it up, and keep it in a cool place.

Anthony Haselmore (1823).

BALM

Balm is a hardy herbaceous perennial which grows wild in many parts of southern England. Its leaves are sweet-scented and possess a refreshing lemon flavour. *Balm* was extensively cultivated in olden times, when it was used as one of the favourite "strewing" herbs, in lieu of carpets. It was also greatly in favour as a flavouring agent for flavouring wines and cordials.

COMPOUND SPIRIT OF BALM

Take of fresh leaves of balm, 8 oz.; lemon peel bruised, 4 oz.; nutmeg and caraway seeds, of each, 2 oz.; cloves, cinnamon and an angelica root, of each, 1 oz. Distil all together with a quart of brandy. It must be well preserved in bottles with ground glass stoppers.

Mrs. Leyel, Herbal Delights.

BALM WINE

Boil forty pounds of sugar in nine gallons of water, for two hours, scum it well, and put it into a tub to cool; take two pounds and a half of the tops of balm, bruise them, and put them into a barrel, with a little new yeast, and when the liquor is cold pour it on the balm, mix it well together, and let it stand four hours, stirring frequently during that time; then close it up, and let it stand six weeks, at the expiration of which rack it off, and put a lump of sugar into every bottle; cork it well and it will be better the second year than the first.

Daily Companion (1799).

BALM WINE

Take a bushel of balm leaves, put them into a tub, and pour eight gallons of scalding water upon them; let it stand a night, then strain it through a hair sieve, and put to every gallon of liquor two pounds of sugar, stirring it very well till the sugar is dissolved; then put it on the fire, adding the whites of four eggs well beaten. When the scum begins to rise, take it off;

26

then let it boil half an hour, skimming it all the time; afterwards put it into the tub again, and when milk-warm add a gill of good ale yeast, stirring it every two hours. Work it thus for two days, then put it into a cask, and bung it up. When fine, bottle it.

J. Davies (1811).

BALM WINE

Boil twenty pounds of lump sugar in four gallons and a half of water gently for an hour, and put it into a tub to cool; bruise two pounds of the tops of green balm, and put them into a barrel with a little new yeast, and when the syrup is nearly cold, pour it on the balm; stir it well together, and let it stand four-and-twenty hours, stirring frequently; bring it up, and when it has stood for six weeks, bottle it, put a lump of sugar into each bottle, and cork tight.

Bishop (1860).

TO MAKE BARLEY WINE

Take half a pound of French barley and boil it in three waters, and save three pints of the last water, and mix it with a quart of white wine, half a pint of borage-water, as much clary-water, a little red rose-water, the juice of five or six lemons, three-quarters of a pound of fine sugar and the thin yellow rind of a lemon; brew all these quick together, run it through a strainer and bottle it up; it is pleasant in hot weather, and very good in fevers.

Gelleroy—London Cook (1762).

EXCELLENT BARLEY-WATER (POOR XURY'S RECEIPT)

Wipe very clean, by rolling it in a soft cloth, two tablespoonfuls of pearl-barley; put it into a quart jug, with a lump or two of sugar, a grain or two of salt, and a strip of lemon-peel, cut thin; fill up the jug with boiling water and keep the mixture gently stirred for some minutes; then cover it down, and let it stand until perfectly cold. In twelve hours, or less, it will be fit for use, but it is better when made overnight. If these directions be followed, the barley-water will be comparatively clear, and very soft and pleasant to drink. A glass of calf's feet jelly added to the barley is an infinite improvement; but as lemon rind is often extremely unpalatable to invalids, their taste should be consulted before that ingredient is added, as it should be also for the degree of sweetness that is desired. After the barley-water has been poured off once, the jug may be filled with boiling water a second time, and even a third time with advantage.

Mrs. Acton (1854).

BARLEY WINE
Boil half a pound of French barley in three waters; save about a pint of the last water, and mix it with a quart of white wine, half a pint of borage water, as much clary water, a little red rose water, the juice of five or six lemons, three-quarters of a pound of sugar, the rind of a lemon; strain and bottle it up.

Bishop (1860).

BIRCH
The birch grows to perfection in the Highlands of Scotland, in Scandinavia, Russia and other northern lands where the vine does not thrive, and in the early spring of the year the birch may be tapped and its sap used for making a cordial wine.

BIRCH WINE
To every gallon of birch water, put 2 lb. of good sugar, boil it half an hour, skim it well, let it stand to settle, then pour it off from the sediment, and put yeast to it, and work it as you do ale 24 hours. Before you tun it, smoke your barrel with brimstone, and to every gallon of liquor, put half a pound of slit raisins. Let it stand 3 or 4 months, then bottle it.

(*MSS. H.101, late eighteenth century.*)

TO MAKE BIRCH WINE
In March bore a hole in a birch-tree, and put in a faucet, and it will run two or three days together without hurting the tree; then put in a pin to stop, and the next year you may draw as much from the same hole; put to every gallon of the liquor a quart of good honey and stir it well together; boil it an hour, skim it well, and put in a few cloves and a piece of lemon-peel, when it is almost cold put to it so much ale-yeast as will make it work like new ale; and when the yeast begins to settle, put it in a runlet that will just hold it; so let it stand six weeks, or longer if you please; then bottle it, and in a month you may

28

drink it; it will keep a year or two; you may make it with sugar, two pounds to a gallon, or something more, if you keep it long; this is admirably wholesome as well as pleasant, an opener of obstructions, good against the phthisis, the spleen and scurvy, a remedy for the stone; it will abate heat in a fever or thrush, and has been given with good success.

Gelleroy—London Cook (1762).

HOW TO MAKE BIRCH WINE

The season for procuring the liquor from the birch-trees is in the beginning of March, while the sap is rising, and before the leaves shoot out, for when the sap is become forward and the leaves begin to appear, the juice, by being long digested in the bark, grows thick and coloured, which was before thin and clear.

The method of procuring the juice is, by boring holes in the body of the tree, and putting in faucets, which are commonly made of the branches of elder, the pitch being taken out; you may, without hurting the trees, if large, tap them in several places, four or five at a time, and by that means, from a good store of trees, save many gallons every day.

If you do not use it immediately, which is the best way, then in order to preserve it in a good condition for brewing, and that it may not turn sour till you have got the quantity you want, the bottle in which it dropped from the faucets, must be immediately well stopped, and the corks waxed or refined.

One method of making it is this, to every gallon of birch liquor put a quart of honey, stir them well together, put in a few cloves and a little lemon peel, and let it boil for near an hour, and scum it well continuously as the scum rises, then set it by to cool, and put in two or three spoonfuls of good ale yeast to set it working, and when the yeast begins to settle, put it in a runlet which will just hold it, and let it stand six weeks, or longer if you please, then bottle it, and it will be fit to drink in a month; it will keep good a year or two. If you have a mind to use sugar instead of honey, put two pounds to a gallon, or more if you would keep it long.

This wine is not only very wholesome, but pleasant; it is a most rich cordial, good in curing consumptions, phthisis, spleen, and also all such inward diseases as accompany the stone in the bladder. Dr. Needham says he has often cured the scurvy

29

with the juice of birch boiled with honey and wine. It is also good to abate heat in a fever.

The British Jewel (1782).

FOR A BIRCH WINE (as made in Sussex)

Take the sap branches, or the top of birch fresh cut, boil it as long as any scum arises : to every gallon of liquor put two pounds of sugar, boil it half an hour, and scum it very clean. When it is almost cold, set it with a little yeast, spread on a toast, as directed in elder wine, let it stand five or six days in an open vessel, stirring it often; then take such a cask as the liquor will be sure to fill; fire three or four large matches dipped in brimstone and put it into the empty cask, and stop the cask till the match is extinguished, always keeping it shook or turned round : take out the ashes, and as quick as possible, pour into it a pint of sack or Rhenish, whichever taste you like best, for the liquor retains it; rinse the cask well with this and pour it out : pour in your wine and stop it close for six months, then if it is perfectly fine you may bottle it.

Daily Companion (1799).

BISHOP
(HOT OR ICED)

The day before the liqueur is wanted, grill on a wire grill, over a clear slow fire, three smooth-skinned large bitter oranges. Grill them of a pale brown. They may be done in an oven, or under a furnace. Place them in a small punch-bowl, that will about hold them, and pour over them a full half-pint from a bottle of old Bordeaux wine, in which a pound and a quarter of loaf sugar is dissolved. Cover with a plate. When it is to be served next day (though it may lie over two or three days), cut and squeeze the oranges into a small sieve placed above a jug, containing the remainder of the bottle of wine previously made very hot. Add more syrup if it is wanted. Serve hot in large glasses; or in summer it may be iced. Bishop is often made of Madeira in England, and perfumed with nutmegs, bruised cloves, and mace. It ought, however, to be made of old generous Bordeaux wine, or it fails of its purpose as a tonic liqueur. It is reckoned highly stomachic, and is served at French dinners, *savans et récherchés*, either as the *coup-d'après* or after the dessert.

Cook and Housewife's Manual (1829).

30

BLACKBERRIES

Blackberries or brambles are among the oldest and greatest English favourites for puddings and pies, jams and jellies, as well as for wines and cordials. They are the fruit of a European thorny bramble which needs no attention at all and grows freely everywhere—much too freely for most people. Blackberries, when ripe and not merely when black, are the finest of all bush berries for juiciness and flavour, in addition to which they are also very cheap, if one lives in the country, as they may be picked without charge from hedgerows in country lanes everywhere during the months of August and September.

WINES OF BLACKBERRIES, STRAWBERRIES, OR DEWBERRIES, HOW TO MAKE THEM

Take of these berries in their proper seasons, moderately ripe, what quantity you please, press them as other berries, boil up water and honey, or water and fine sugar, as your palate best relishes, to considerable sweetness; and when it is well scummed put the juice in, and let it simmer to incorporate it well with the water, and when it has done so, take it off, let it cool, and scum it again, then put it up in a barrel, or rather a close glazed earthen vessel ; to ferment and settle, put then to every gallon half a pint of Malaga, and draw it off, as clear as may be ; bottle it up, and keep it cool for use.

Their virtues. These liquors are agreeably good in fevers, afflictions of the lungs, prevent the infection of pestilential airs, get a good appetite, and much help digestion, excellent in surfeits and cause good blood.

The Way to Get Wealth (1706).

BLACKBERRY WINE

To every gallon of ripe blackberries, add one gallon of boiling water (let the berries be well bruised before the water be put to them), then let them stand twenty-four hours, stirring them about twice or thrice a day; after that run the liquor through a hair sieve, and to every gallon of it put two pound and a half of powdered sugar (or a good clean natural sugar). Let it stand twenty-four hours more in the vessel unstopped, stirring it up now and then; afterwards close it up well, and let it remain thus for three months, then draw it off into a clean vessel, with a lump of sugar put into it. Stop it up close, and in a week's time if you see it be fine enough, you may bottle it off.

This blackberry wine (as I have elsewhere remarked) if it be well made, and allowed a due time to ripen, and deposit its more fixed and earthy parts, comes the nearest in taste and goodness to French Claret of any that can be produced from our own vegetable growth; but then the juice must not be too much diluted with water; for it may be accounted as a general rule, that the more this and the like juices are let down with water, the weaker and worse tasted do their wines become. Therefore I think the same proportion of water prescribed in the foregoing gooseberry wine, may be sufficient here, considering that the quantity of sugar is also less in this, than in the other; which for any reason that I can see, ought to be nearly equal. Therefore I have annexed the following prescription, which affords a strong, well-bodied wine, not inferior to the best claret.

Take to every three quarts of blackberries, two quarts of spring water, boil the water and let it stand till it be cold; then put it upon the berries in a stand for eight hours, afterward draw off the liquor while it will run clear, and strain the rest through a jelly-bag; and to every gallon of this liquor put three pounds of good sugar; barrel it close up; and at the end of three months, clear it from the settlement (which filter through a bag); clean the cask, and put your wine in it again, with a lemon sliced, adding to each gallon of wine half a pound of loaf sugar; then let it stand till March, and bottle it off.

As this is an excellent well tasted wine, so also is it taken to be somewhat medicinal, being reckoned by many as a specific for the piles; and there is now living a reverend gentleman who assured me that he hath more than once freed himself from the danger of a fistula, which he had cause to be apprehensive of, by only drinking this wine daily for a considerable space of time. Yet whether this person's case was really such as he apprehended, is what I dare not venture to determine; although I am inclined to think it was from the experiments of many who have tried the happy effects of it. And it is what Hippocrates himself, *De morb. mulier, pag.* 199, doth commend for healing ulcers and excrescences arising near the pudendum. The stipticity and austerity of this fruit, which it retains, even after fermentation, may likewise recommend it as a good astringent; equal in all cases, perhaps, to foreign red wines.

The Practical Distiller (1734).

TO MAKE BLACKBERRY WINE

Let your berries be full ripe when you gather them, put them into a large vessel, either of wood or stone, with a cock in it, and pour upon them as much boiling water as will cover them : as soon as the heat will permit you to put your hand into the vessel, bruise them well, till all the berries are broken, then let them stand covered till the berries begin to rise towards the top, which they will do in three or four days; then draw off the clear liquor into another vessel, and add to every ten quarts of this liquor one pound of sugar, stir it well in it, and let it stand to work a week or ten days in another vessel like the first; then draw it off at the cock, through a jelly-bag, into a large vessel, take four ounces of isinglass, and lay it to steep twelve hours in a pint of white wine, the next morning boil it upon a slow fire till it is all dissolved; then take a gallon of your blackberry juice, put in the dissolved isinglass, give them a boil together, and pour all into the vessel, let it stand a few days to purge and settle; then draw it off, and keep it in a cool place.

Daily Companion (1799).

BRAMBLE WINE (Mrs. Hall's, 21st Feb., '38)

Take 1 quart of brambles, full ripe and bruised, 1 quart of water, stand 12 hours. Strain through a sieve and to every gallon of liquor add 2½ lb. of moist sugar—dissolve and put the liquor into a clean cask. To every 2 gallons put 2d. of isinglass, and bung it down next day.

Duncan Macdonald, New London Family Cook (c. 1800).

TO MAKE BLACKBERRY WINE

Gather your berries when they are full ripe, take twelve quarts, and crush them with your hand, boil six gallons of water with twelve pounds of brown sugar a quarter of an hour, scum it well, then pour it on the blackberries, and let it stand all night, then strain it through a hair sieve, put into your cask six pounds of Malaga raisins a little cut, then put the wine into the cask with one ounce of isinglass, which must be dissolved in a little cider, stir it all up together, close it up, and let it stand six months, and then bottle it.

English Housekeeper (1806).

CAPILLAIRE, TO MAKE

Take fourteen pounds of sugar, three pounds of coarse sugar, six eggs beaten in with the shells, three quarts of water; boil it up twice, skim it well, then add to it a quarter of a pint of orange flower water; strain it through a jelly-bag, and put it in bottles when cold; mix a spoonful or two of this syrup, as it is liked for sweetness, in a draught of warm or cold water.

Bishop (1860).

CARAWAY SEEDS

The seeds of the *Carum Carvi*, an umbelliferous plant which grows wild in many parts of England and should be cultivated in every kitchen-garden; its roots and leaves are excellent as a vegetable, or in sauces, soups and stews; whilst its seeds may be used to great advantage to give bread and pastry a very pleasant taste as well as to flavour all sorts of drinks, chiefly a liqueur which is one of the most popular of all liqueurs, *Kummel*, the German name for caraway.

CARAWAY

For three gallons, take seven quarts of rectified malt spirit, three pennyweights of the oil of caraway, two ounces of cassia, two pounds of loaf sugar, one gill of spirit of wine, and fill up with water. The cassia and caraway seeds must be well pounded, and steeped for three or four days in a quart of the spirit, and the oil must be killed the same way as for the gin; fine and work it also the same.

J. Davies (1811).

CHERRIES

The many hundred varieties of cultivated cherries may be roughly divided into two main families, sour and sweet. All wines, cordials and liqueurs made from cherries are made from one or the other of the various species which belong to the sour group, all of which are more juicy than the sweet or dessert cherries. The first favourite among cherries used for the making of English wines has always been the black Morello, chiefly on account of its dark juice, from which a beverage can be fermented, in colour, not unlike a light claret. The favourite cherry for the making of liqueurs is the Damasca, a small and very dark cherry from Dalmatia, where it is used in the making

34

of Maraschino. In England, however, cherry brandy and cherry cordials are mostly made from the fermented juice of red or black Morello cherries, distilled and suitably sweetened.

THE COUNTESS OF NEWPORT'S CHERRY WINE

Pick the best cherries free from rotten, and pick the stalks from them; put them into an earthen pan. Bruise them, by gripping and straining them in your hands, and let them stand all night; on the next day strain them out (through a napkin; which if it be a coarse and thin one, let the juice run through a hippocras or jelly-bag, upon a pound of fine pure sugar in powder to every gallon of juice) and to every gallon put a pound of sugar, and put it into a vessel. Be sure your vessel be full or your wine will be spoiled; you must let it stand a month before you bottle it : and in every bottle you must put a lump (a piece as big as a nutmeg) of sugar. The vessel must not be stopped until it hath done working.

Sir Kenelme Digby (1669).

MORELLO WINE

To half an Aume of white wine, take twenty pounds of Morello cherries, the stalks being first picked off. Bruise the cherries and break the stones. Pour in the wine the juice that comes out from the cherries, but put all the solid substance of them into a long bag of boulter cloth, and hang it in the wine at the bung, so that it lie not in the bottom, but only reach to touch it, and therefore nail it down at the mouth of the bung. Then stop it close. For variety, you may put some clear juice of cherries alone (but drawn from a larger proportion of cherries) into another parcel of wine. To either of them, if you will aromatise the drink, take to this quantity two ounces of cinnamon broken and bruised and put it in a little bag at the spigot, that all the wine you draw may run through the cinnamon. You must be careful in bruising the cherries, and breaking the stones. For if you do all at once, the liquor will sparkle about. But you must first bruise the cherries gently in a mortar, and rub through a sieve all that will pass, and strain the residue hard through your hands. Then beat the remaining hard, so strongly as may break all the stones. Then put all together, and strain them clean through a strainer, and put the solider substance into the bag to hang in the wine.

Sir Kenelme Digby (1669).

THE CORDIAL CHERRY WATER

Take nine pounds of red cherries, nine pints of claret wine, eight ounces of cinnamon, three ounces of nutmegs; bruise your spice, stone your cherries, and steep them in the wine, then add to them half a handful of rosemary, half a handful of balm, one quarter of a handful of sweet marjoram, let them steep in an earthen pot twenty-four hours, and as you put them into the alembeck, to distil them, bruise them with your hands, and make a soft fire under them, and distil by degrees; you may mix the waters at your pleasure when you have drawn them all; when you have thus done, sweeten it with loaf sugar, then strain it into another glass, and stop it close that no spirits go out; you may (if you please) hang a bag with musk and ambergris in it, when you use it, mix it with syrup of gilly-flowers or of violets, as you best like it; it is an excellent cordial for fainting fits, or a woman in travail, or for any one who is not well.

Queen-like Closet, Hannah Wolley (1672).

HOW TO MAKE WINE-ROYAL OF RED CHERRIES

Press out as much juice from the cherries as you can, and then stamp the stones with the skins to a mash, breaking all the stones; for you cannot stamp them before you press out the juice of them, by reason the juice will spatter about; then put the juice with the stones and skins into an open vessel, and stir it well about, and let it stand two or three days, that the liquor may draw out the tincture and cordial part of the skins and the corroborating virtue of the kernels; then press it out, and put it into a cask, and let it stand until it begin to be clear, which may be in a fortnight's time; then rack it off from the gross lees into a clean, dry and sweet cask, and put into every gallon of it a pint of good spirit, and a pint and a half of the syrup or sweets. Stir it well together with a staff for a quarter of an hour, then stop it up close for about a quarter of a year, and then you may bottle it. A glass of this excellent wine-royal of cherries, drank half an hour before meals, procures a good appetite; and after meals, helps digestion; it is cordial, cheers the heart, revives the spirits; it is diuretic and admirably provokes brine, and carries with it sand and gravel out of the reins and bladder, and all such foul and ill matters out of the body that offends the head, stomach and belly. And the wine made of currants and gooseberries are highly commended by the learned Dr. Willis to be very wholesome, and good for the liver, and against the scurvy by sweetening the blood.

The Family Physitian (1696).

TO MAKE WINE-ROYAL OF BLACK CHERRIES

Having pressed out as much of the juice as you can from the cherries, stamp the stones and skins as you did with the red cherries, keep the juice apart, put the skins and stones in a vessel, and pour upon it scalding hot water, stir it well together and cover it up close, let it stand two days; that the hot water may extract all the tincture out of the skins and the cephalic and corroborating virtue of the kernels; then press it out, and put this liquor with the juice of the cherries into a cask, and after a fortnight rack off from the gross lees into another clean dry cask, and put into it the same quantity of spirits and syrup as is directed in making the other royal-wines.

This wine of black cherries has an admirable cephalic virtue; it is excellent against the vertigo or dizziness and swimming in the head. The reason why you put water to the stamped cherries is because the juice of the black cherries is a very thick and sweet juice, and would not extract the tincture and virtue out of the skins and kernels, as the juice of the red cherries will do. The quantity of water you use, is the same with that in making the royal-wine of currants and gooseberries.

The Family Physitian (1696).

WINE OF CHERRIES

Take cherries indifferently ripe, of any red sort, clear them of the stalks and stones, and then put them into an earthen glazed vessel, and with your clean hands squeeze them to pulp, or you may do it with a wooden ladle, or presser, and so let them continue twelve hours to ferment, then put them into a linen cloth not too fine, and press out the juice with a pressing-board, or any other conveniency, then let the liquor stand till the scum arise; and with your ladle take it clean off, then pour out the clearer part by inclination into a cask, where to each gallon put a pound of the best loaf sugar, and let it ferment, and purge seven or eight days, so draw it off, when you find it clear, into lesser casks, or bottles, keep it cool, as other wines, and in ten or twelve days it will be ripe.

Its Virtues. This is a great cooler of the body, in the heat of weather, cheers the heart, and much enlivens nature in its decay; it is good against violent pains in the head, and swooning fits.

The Way to get Wealth (1706).

MORELLO WINE

Take two gallons of white wine, and twenty pounds of Morello cherries, take away the stalks, and so bruise them that the stones may be broken, press the juice into the wine, put mace, cinnamon and nutmeg, each an ounce, in a bag grossly bruised, hang it in the wine when you have put it up in a cask; and it will be a rich drink.

The Way to get Wealth (1706).

MORELLO CHERRY WINE

Let your cherries be very ripe, pick off the stalks, and bruise your fruit without breaking the stones; put them in an open vessel together; let them stand twenty-four hours; then press them, and to every gallon put two pounds of fine sugar; then put it up in your cask, and when it has done working stop it up close; let it stand three or four months and bottle it; it will be fit to drink in two months.

Gelleroy—London Cook (1762).

BLACK CHERRY WINE

Boil six gallons of spring water an hour, then bruise twenty-four pounds of black cherries, but do not break the stones; pour the water boiling hot on the cherries, stir the cherries well in the water, and let it stand twenty-four hours, then strain it off, and to every gallon put near two pounds of good sugar, mix it well with the liquor, and let it stand one day longer, then pour it off clear into the vessel, and stop it up close. Let it be very fine before you draw it off into bottles.

The British Jewel (1782).

ANOTHER WAY TO MAKE CHERRY WINE, TO TASTE OF THE KERNEL

When your red cherries are full ripe, strip them from the sprigs, and stamp them as apples, till the stones are broke, put it into a tub, and cover it close for three days, and nights; press them in a cider-press, and put your liquor again into a tub, and let it stand close covered two days more, then take the scum very carefully off, pour it off the lees into another tub, and be very careful not to shake the vessel, and let it stand to clear two days more, then scum and pour it off as before; if your cherries are ripe and sweet, put only a pound and a half of moist Lisbon sugar to each gallon of liquor, stir it well together and cover it close next day, then pour it carefully off the lees as before; let it stand again and do the same the next day into the vessel you keep it in. You may repeat this oftener if you see the lees are gross and like to make it fret; when it is settled stop it up for seven or eight months, then if it is perfectly fine, bottle it; if not draw it off into another vessel, and stop it up for three weeks longer. This wine keeps seven years, if bottled; it is not fit to drink until it has been six months in bottle.

Our English wines want only age to equal, if not exceed, all foreign liquors.

Daily Companion (1799).

TO MAKE BLACK CHERRY WINE

Take the largest sort of black cherries, pick off the stalks and put them into a tub. Then take a kettle of water, and make it boil till it is half consumed, then take as much of the water as will cover the cherries. Then cover them with a linen or woollen cloth to keep in the steam and let them stand all night. The next day strain them through a straining sieve, without bruising them as that will make the wine thick. Then take out the cherries that were strained and put more water to them and boil them together till the strength be boiled out of them. Then strain them through sieve to the other juice. Then boil all the liquor a quarter of an hour together and skim it clean. Then put to every gallon of liquor ¾ lb. sugar. Then boil all together another quarter of an hour. Then set to cool as you do ale. Then put barm to it to make it work. Then turn it into a vessel and keep it filled up till it has done working. Stop it up and in two months or thereabouts you may bottle it out.

MS. Book of Recipes. C1

BLACK CHERRY BRANDY

Stone eight pounds of black cherries, and put them to a gallon of brandy. Bruise the stones, and put them in, cover

39

them up close, and let them stand five or six weeks. Then pour it clear from the sediments, and bottle it. Morello cherries, done in this manner, make a fine rich cordial.

Anthony Hazelmore (1823).

CHERRY BRANDY

Choose the finest morel cherries you can obtain; place them in layers in glass jars, strew pounded sugar between each layer, cover them with brandy. As soon as the cherries have imbibed the brandy, pour in more, so as to keep them constantly covered.

Bishop (1860).

CINNAMON

The cinnamon tree is grown in both the East and West Indies for the sake of its bark, which possesses marked antiseptic and cleansing properties, as well as a pungent clove-like smell.

CINNAMON BRANDY

Bruise 3 oz. of cinnamon bark and put it into a bottle of good French brandy and leave it for two or three weeks before using it. It will prove, in most cases, an excellent remedy to cure a cold, if added in no miserly manner to hot milk. It may also be used to prevent a cold in either hot milk or hot water : if used in hot water, sugar should be added.

CORRELLAS, OR CINNAMON

To four bottles of brandy, put four ounces of cinnamon, thirty cloves, thirteen coriander seeds, and a little salt; mix all together in a little brandy; infuse it for eighteen hours; take as much from the still as you can; put two pounds of clarified sugar in two quarts of water, with the whites of two eggs, well beaten together; mix it with the spirit, and filter it through blotting paper. Cork your bottles well.

Duncan Macdonald, New London Family Cook (c. 1800).

CITRON

There is a citron tree (*Citrus medica*), and the peel of its fruit is used by French confectioners, to whom it is known as *Cédrat*. But the citron wine and citron cordial made in England in the past were not made from the fruit of the Citron tree : they were made from lemons and called citron for no better reason than that *citron* is the French name for lemon.

CITRON WINE

Pare 18 lemons, and as many oranges very thin; let the peel steep 24 hours in a gallon of brandy close stopped. Take 6 quarts of water, and 3 lb. loaf sugar clarified with the whites of six eggs. Let them boil half an hour, skim it and let it stand till cold; then put it with the brandy and a quart of juice of oranges and lemons (or more if you think proper) into a vessel suitable for the quantity you make; stop it up till fine, which will be in about 5 or 6 weeks; if at that time it is not very fine, or is too sweet, let it stand longer before you bottle it. Orange leaves or small green fruit put into the vessel tied in a muslin bag is a great advantage to the wine.

N.B.—If you choose, you may tun up the parings of the oranges and lemons with the wine.

CITRON CORDIAL

For three gallons, take seven quarts of spirits, twelve pounds of figs, four pounds of prunes, two pennyweights of the oil of orange, three pennyweights of the essence of lemon, ten drops of the oil of cloves, two pounds of sugar. Fill up with water.

N.B.—The figs and prunes must be bruised, and steeped in the spirit for eight or ten days. Kill the oils and essence the same as for gin. Most people choose to have citron of a pale green colour; to make which, boil some spinage, and squeeze the juice into your citron.

ANOTHER WAY

To one gallon of brandy, or malt spirit, take ten citrons; pare off the outer rinds, and dry them well in the sun, then beat the remaining part of the citrons to a mash in a mortar, and put it into the brandy, stop it close, and let it stand nine or ten days; then draw off the liquor clean from the bottoms into another bottle, and take the rinds that are dry, beat them to powder and infuse them nine days in the spirit; after which draw it off into a clean bottle, and sweeten it to your taste with loaf sugar; then bottle it.

J. Davies (1811).

CLARY

An English herb of the sage family (*Salvia sclarea*), which was reputed to be particularly useful to relieve eye soreness:

hence its name clary, or "clear eye." It used to be added to some of the English wines, for the sake of the slight sage-like flavour which it imparted to the wine, and maybe also because of its mucilage, which may have acted as "finings" and helped to "clear" the wine.

TO MAKE CLARY WINE
Pick twenty-four pounds of Malaga raisins, and chop them very small; then put them into a tub, and to each pound put a quart of water; let them steep ten or eleven days, stirring it twice every day, and be careful to keep it covered; then strain it off and put it into a vessel, with about half a peck of the tops of clary, when it is in blossom; stop it close for six weeks, and then bottle it off; in two or three months it will be fit for drinking.

Daily Companion (1799).

CLARY WINE
I
Pick twenty-four pounds of Malaga raisins, and chop them very small, then put them into a tub, and to each pound allow a quart of water; let them steep twelve days, stirring them twice a day, and taking care to keep it well covered; then strain it off, and put it into a clean cask, with about half a peck of the tops of clary, when in blossom. Afterwards bung it up for six weeks, and then bottle it. In two months, it will be fit to drink. As there will be a good deal of sediment, it will be necessary to tap pretty high.

II
Take ten gallons of water, twenty-five pounds of sugar, and the whites of twelve eggs well beaten; set it over the fire and let it boil gently for an hour, skimming it frequently; then put it into a tub, and when almost cool put it into your cask, with about half a peck of clary tops and a pint of ale yeast. Stir it three times a day, for three days, and when it has done working close it up, if fine you may bottle it in about four months.

J. Davies (1811).

CLARY WINE
Boil fifteen gallons of water, with forty-five pounds of sugar, skim it, when cool put a little to a quarter of a pint of yeast, and so by degrees add a little more. In an hour pour the small

42

quantity to the large, pour the liquor on clary-flowers picked in the dry; the quantity for the above is twelve quarts. Those who gather from their own garden, may have not sufficient to put in at once, and may add as they can get them, keeping account of each quart. When it has ceased to hiss and the flowers are all in, stop it up for four months. Rack it off, empty the barrel of the dregs, and adding a gallon of the best brandy, stop it up, and let it stand six or eight weeks, then bottle it.

Domestic Cookery (1814).

CLARY WINE

Pick twenty-four pounds of Malaga raisins, and chop them : then put them into a tub, and to each pound put a quart of water. Let them steep ten or twelve days, stirring it twice each day, and keep it close covered. Then strain it off, and put it into a vessel, with about half a peck of the tops of clary, when it is in blossom. Stop it close for six weeks, and then bottle it off. In two or three months it will be fit for drink.

Anthony Haselmore (1823).

CLOVES

Cloves are the dried unexpanded flower-buds or partly formed seeds of the clove tree, a very beautiful tree of the myrtle family, which grows best in the Moluccas. Cloves are the most stimulating of all the aromatic spices, and they have been used—and are still used—extensively as a flavouring agent for both food and drink.

CLOVE CORDIAL

For three gallons, take two gallons of rectified malt spirit, half a pound of clove pepper, two pennyweights of the oil of cloves, one pint of elder juice, one pound and a half of loaf sugar. Fill up with water. To colour it, put some archil in a bag, and press it into the spirit till it becomes a deep red, and let it fine of itself. If you choose it white, leave out the elder juice and archil, and fine it the same way as gin.

CORDIAL WATER

Take lavender-cotton, horehound, wormwood and fetherfew, of each three handsful; rice, peppermint, and Seville orange-peel, of each one handful. Mix them together, and steep them all night in red wine, or the bottoms of strong beer. Then

43

distil them pretty quick in a hot still, and it will be a fine cordial to take as bitters.

Anthony Haselmore (1823).

CORIANDER

An Eastern plant with parsley-like leaves : it was introduced in England by the Romans, and is occasionally met in the Eastern Counties, growing wild near rivers or in wet fields. It is cultivated commercially in Essex for the sake of its seeds, which become fragrant when dried and retain their spicy smell for a considerable time. Coriander seeds are used to flavour gin and other spirits.

CORIANDER CORDIAL

For three gallons, take seven quarts of rectified malt spirit, two pounds of coriander seed, one ounce of caraway seed, six drops of the oil of orange, two pounds of sugar. Fill up with water.

N.B.—The coriander and caraway seeds must be bruised and steeped in the spirit for ten or twelve days, and well stirred two or three times a day. Fine it the same as you do gin.

J. Davies (1811).

COWSLIP

One of the prettiest and commonest of wild flowers to greet the return of Spring in fields and copses all over England. They were, once upon a time, very popular for making English wines, probably because there was such an abundant supply available, rather than on account of their distinctive flavour, which is not unpleasant, but by no means remarkable.

TO MAKE COWSLIP WINE

Take six gallons of water and ten pounds of sugar, boil them together for half an hour; set it to cool, when it is almost cold put into it two or three spoonfuls of yeast well beaten with the juice of sixteen lemons; then put in also a peck and a half of cowslip flowers beaten in a stone mortar, let them work together for two or three days; then press it out, and strain it and put it in a cask, which must be full of it; stop it but loosely till you perceive it has done working, then stop it up close and after a month bottle it.

The Family Physitian (1696).

COWSLIP WINE

Put five pounds of loaf sugar to four gallons of fair water, simmer them over a fire half an hour to well dissolve the sugar, and when it is taken off, and cold, put in half a peck of cowslip flowers clean picked, and gently bruised, then put two spoonfuls of new ale yeast, and a pound of syrup of lemons beaten with it, with a lemon-peel or two, and so in a well-seasoned cask or vessel let them stand close stopped for three days that they may ferment well, then put in some juice of cowslips, and give it a convenient space to work, and when it has stood a month draw it off into bottles, putting a little lump of loaf sugar into each, and so you may well keep it the space of a year; and thus you may make wine of such other like flowers that are of pleasant taste and scent, as oxlips, jessamine, peachblooms, comfry, scabeous, fetherfew, fumitary, and a number more, as your fancy leads you, for I have shewed you different ways to let you know that you need not exactly keep to one certain rule, but please your palate by such additions as you think convenient, though by straying too far, you may happen to mar the whole design; therefore, in all things, keep as near as you can to the rules I have given.

Its virtues. Cowslip wine moderately drunk much helps the palsy, cramp, convulsions and all other diseases of the nerves and sinews; also eases pains of the joints and gout, and contributes mainly to the curing of ruptures.

The Way to get Wealth (1706).

TO MAKE COWSLIP WINE

To six gallons of water put fourteen pounds of sugar, stir it well together, and beat the whites of twenty eggs very well, and mix it with the liquor, and make it boil as fast as possible; skim it well, and let it continue boiling two hours; then strain it through a hair sieve, and set it to cool; and when it is as cold as wort should be, put a small quantity of yeast to it on a toast, or in a dish; let it stand all night working; then bruise a peck of cowslip, put them into your vessel, and your liquor upon them, adding six ounces of syrup of lemons; cut a turf of grass and lay on the bung; let it stand a fortnight, and then bottle it; put your tap into your vessel before you put your wine in, that you may not shake it.

Gelleroy—London Cook (1762).

45

TO MAKE COWSLIP, PRIMROSE, OR GILLYFLOWER WINE

To every gallon of water take 2 lb. of the best powdered sugar. Boil it an hour and skim it clean, and put to cool. To every gallon of liquor an ounce and a half of syrup of citron or lemon. And to 10 gallons 2 spoonfuls of Ale-yeast beaten with the syrup, put together working, having two toasts spread with the yeast and the syrup. Set them working two days; while working put in the flowers being stamped.

To 10 gallons you must put in half a bushel of cowslip or primrose flowers (and of gillyflowers a peck into the same quantity), put in 2 lemons, rind and all chopped, and a pottle of white wine. Put all those in the working together. When it has stood a month or six weeks bottle it up, putting a lump of sugar in every bottle.

MS. C6 (early nineteenth century).

CURACAO

The earliest and still the best form of orange liqueur. It was first made in Holland, being sweetened with West Indian cane sugar and flavoured with the rind of a species of Orange (*Citrus Aurantium curassuviensis*) from Curaçao or Curaçoa, a Dutch West Indian island some 40 miles off the north coast of Venezuela.

CURACAO

To a pint of the best rectified spirit, add four ounces of spirit of orange peel, and one pint clarified syrup.

French brandy may be used in preference to the spirits. It is an admirable cordial, and a great improvement to punch.

Indian Domestic Economy (1849).

CURRANTS

The name applies to three distinct types of fruit, all of them used for making both wines and cordials.

1. Black currants (*Ribes nigrum*) are the fruit of a European bush tree which has been cultivated in England for a considerable time. Not only its little black berries but its green leaves have a very distinctive and pungent smell and taste.

2. Red currants (*Ribes sativum*), and their albino form, the white currants, are one and the same fruit which merely differ in skin colouring. They were introduced in England a long while ago, but at a much more recent date than the black cur-

rants, which they do not resemble at all as regards flavour an taste.

3. Currants, the name given in England to small seedless raisins from the Levant, and originally obtained from Corinth, hence their name.

CURRANT WINE

Take a pound of the best Currants clean picked, and pour upon them in a deep straight-mouthed earthen vessel six pounds or pints of hot water, in which you have dissolved three spoonfuls of the purest and newest ale-yeast. Stop it very close till it ferment, then give such vent as is necessary, and keep it warm for about three days, it will work and ferment. Taste it after two days, to see if it be grown to your liking. As soon as you find it so, let it run through a strainer, to leave behind all the exhausted currants and the yeast, and so bottle it up. It will be exceeding quick and pleasant, and is admirable good to cool the liver, and cleanse the blood. It will be ready to drink in five or six days after it is bottled; and you may drink safely large draughts of it.

Sir Kenelme Digby (1669).

RED CURRANT WINE

Take your currants, being full ripe, and crush them with your hands; there is no occasion to strip them from the stalks; then strain your juice through a sieve, and to every pint thereof (being first boiled and cooled again) add near one pint of water. To every gallon of this liquor, put three pounds of good fine sugar, let it stand to dissolve twenty-four hours (often stirring it about). Then tun it in a suitable cask, and when the working is over, close it up, and let it stand for three months. When you bottle it, put a lump of loaf sugar into each bottle. This will make the wine drink brisker, and sparkle much finer, than when it is omitted. It hath been surmised by some understanding persons, that if the loaf sugar be powdered, it will not be so effectual; as they suppose the pores of the sugar to contain a quantity of air which by reason of its elastic and expansive nature, causes that additional fermentation, as soon as it is set at liberty, by the removal of the cork or stopper.

But when the sugar comes to be powdered, and its pores destroyed by that means, they think it must become ineffectual and useless. But this does not always hold good; for there is scarce any country housewife, who knows not how to recover her ale, or beer, when upon the fret or pricking, by bottling it immediately up, with a lump of such sugar as she has at hand; which being well corked down, and suffered to rest so for some time, the liquor will afterwards recover itself, and appear brisk, lively, and well-tasted : yet I do not deny, but that loaf sugar is the better when it is to be had; but in country places, where it may happen to be deficient, the other may well enough supply its place, where the colour of the liquor does not forbid it.

The Practical Distiller (1734).

HOW TO MAKE CURRANT WINE

Gather your currants full ripe, strip them and bruise them in a mortar, and to every gallon of the pulp put two quarts of water, first boiled and cold (you may put in some grapes if you please) let it stand in a tub twenty-four hours to ferment, then let it run through a hair sieve, let no hand touch it, let it take its time to run, and to every gallon of this liquor, put two pounds and a half of white sugar; stir it well and put it in your vessel, and to every six gallons put in a quart of the best rectified spirits of wine. Let it stand six weeks and bottle it. If it is not very fine, empty it into other bottles, and after it has stood a fortnight rack it off into smaller.

The British Jewel (1782).

MR. PALMER'S RECEIPT FOR CURRANT WINE

Pick the currants from the stalks, and squeeze them. Mix one gallon of juice with two gallons of spring water, put 11 or 12 lb. of loaf sugar to each such quantity with some juice of raspberries drawn off with loaf sugar. Let the sugar and water be put together first and then the currant juice. Let it stand to work then put it in the cask first putting in 2 quarts of brandy and when it has done hissing 3 quarts to every 10 gallons of wine. Bung it very secure first putting into the cask some sheets of writing paper torn in small pieces to fine it down. You may draw it off in April following but better to be deferred longer.

MS. Book of Recipes. F2 (1805)

TO MAKE BLACK CURRANT WINE

To a gallon of water, put four pounds of black currants;

48

boil them together half an hour; then strain it, and to every gallon of the liquor, put four pounds of loaf sugar; boil it, and scum it; when cool, work it with a little yeast, and to every gallon, put a pint of raspberries, and the same of red currants, that have been boiled up with sugar : put all into the barrel, and let it stand twelve months, then bottle it.

N.B.—The older it is the better. It should not be drank before it is two years old.

Addison Ashburn (1807).

TO MAKE WHITE CURRANT WINE

To every gallon of water, put five pounds of the best Lisbon sugar, and five pounds of currants, with the stalks; let the water be well boiled, and stand till cold; then put it into the barrel, with the fruit, and stop it up in ten days or a fortnight. Bottle it the first week in December.

Addison Ashburn (1807)

DAMSONS

Damsons belong to a race of small rounded plums, deep blue in the skin, with greenish flesh or pulp. They are closely related to the sloes of the hedgerows, although they are regarded as being allied to or descended from the Damascus plumtree, *Prunus institia*, and are sometimes called *Damascenes*.

WINE OF PLUMS, DAMSONS, ETC.

To do this, take what plums you please, mix those of a sweet taste with an allay of those that are somewhat sour, though they must all be inclining to ripeness, slit them in halves, so that the stones may be taken out, then mash them gently, and add a little water and honey the better to moisten them; boil to every gallon of pulp of your plums, a gallon of spring-water, in it a few bay-leaves and cloves, add as much sugar as will well sweeten it, scum off the froth, and let it cool, then press the fruit, squeezing out the liquid part, strain all through a fine strainer, and put the water and juice up together in a cask, let it stand and ferment three or four days, fine it with white sugar, flour and whites of eggs, and draw it off into bottles, so corking it up that the air may not prejudice it, and in ten or twelve days it will be ripe, and taste like sherry, if not a nearer flavour of Canary.

Damsons may be ordered as other plums, though they produce a tarter wine, more clear and longer lasting, but put not so much water to them, as to luscious plums, unless you mix some sweet wine with it, as Malaga, Canary or the like, or infuse raisins of the sun in it, which will give it a rich and mellow taste.

Their virtues. These, as other wines made of English fruit, are moderately cooling, purify the blood, and cleanse the reins, cause a freeness of urine, and contribute much to soft slumbers and a quiet rest, by sending up gentle refreshing spirits to the brain, which dispel heat and noxious vapours thence, and put that noble part into a right temperature.

The Way to get Wealth (1706).

TO MAKE DAMSON WINE

Gather your damsons dry, weigh them, and bruise them with your hand; put them into an earthen stein that has a faucet, put a wreath of straw before the faucet; to every eight pounds of fruit a gallon of water; boil the water, skim it, and put it to your fruit scalding hot, let it stand two whole days; then draw it off, and put it into a vessel fit for it, and to every gallon of liquor put two pounds and a half of fine sugar; let the vessel be full, and stop it close; the longer it stands the better; it will keep a year in the vessel; bottle it out; the small damson is the best; you may put a very small lump of double refined sugar in every bottle.

Gelleroy—London Cook (1724).

A RECEIPT FOR DAMSON WINE

To every gallon of water put two pounds and a half of sugar which you must boil and scum three-quarters of an hour; and to every gallon put five pints of damsons, with the stones taken away; let them boil till it is of a fine colour, then strain it through a fine sieve. Work it in an open vessel three or four days, then pour it off the lees, and let it work in that vessel as long as it will. Stop it up for six or eight months; when, if fine, you may bottle it, and it will keep a year or two in bottles.

Daily Companion (1799).

DAMSON WINE

To three pecks of damsons put ten gallons of boiling water, cover it close and le: it stand three days then draw it off, and to every gallon of liquor put three pounds of good moist sugar, then boil it half an hour, taking off the scum as it rises. Put it in a tub when cold, add a little yeast upon toasted bread and let it stand two days, put it in the cask with 5 lb. of raisins chopped. When it has done fermenting put one quart of best brandy with one ounce of isinglass dissolved in a little wine. It will be ready to bottle in four months.

MS. Book of Recipes A2 (1833).

DANDELION

The dandelion is one of the commonest of European weeds; it is a curse in many gardens, but it is also extensively cultivated in many parts of Europe, as well as in Asia and North America for the sake of its bitter root and leaves. In England, the buds and flowers of the dandelion were used to make dandelion wine or dandelion beer, for their flavour and probably even more for their stimulating action upon the kidneys.

DANDELION BEER

3½ quarts of dandelions to 1 gallon of water, boil half an hour, strain. 3 lb. of moist sugar to 1 gallon of liquor, boil half an hour, skim well, then put into a tub until cool. 1 lemon, 1 orange, 1 pennyworth of yeast, put all together into cask, stir every day for a fortnight, then bung up, in six weeks it is ready to bottle. In addition to the above I use bruised ginger ½ lb., cowslips 12 quarts, raisins 3 lb. for 12 gallons, ginger to be boiled before put into barrel, rest to go in at once.

MS. Book of Recipes A4 (1833).

TO MAKE EBULUM

To a hogshead of strong ale take a heaped bushel of elder-berries, and half a pound of juniper berries beaten; put in all the berries, when you put in the hops, and let them boil together till the berries break in pieces, then work it up as you do ale; when it has done working, add to it half a pound of ginger, half an ounce of cloves, as much mace, an ounce of nutmegs, as much cinnamon, grossly beaten, half a pound of citron, as much eringo root, and likewise of candied orange-peel; let the sweet-meats be cut in pieces very thin, and put with the spice into a

bag, and hang it in the vessel when you stop it up; so let it stand till it is fine, then bottle it up, and drink it with lumps of double refined sugar in the glass.
Gelleroy—London Cook (1762).

ELDER

The elder is a widely distributed European tree which thrives remarkably well in most parts of the British Isles. It bears an abundance of clusters of white flowers soon to be followed by small black berries, both the flowers and fruit being used to make English wines and cordials. Elder flowers are used as a flavouring agent : they impart to wine so distinct a "muscatel" flavour that they are used for flavouring some of the still and sparkling wines which are supposed to have been made from muscatel grapes. Elderberries have long been among the first favourites for the making of English wines, not only because they were plentiful and inexpensive, but also on account of the deep colour of their juice. The wine had the reputation of being just like port, but only to look at, of course.

TO MAKE THE ELDER WATER, OR SPIRIT OF SAMBUCUS

Take some rye leaven, and break it small into some warm water, let it be a sour one, for that is best; about two ounces or more; then take a bushel of elder berries beaten small, and put them into an earthen pot and mix them very well with the leaven, and let it stand one day near the fire; then put in a little yeast, and stir it well together to make it rise, so let it stand ten days covered, and sometimes stir it; then distil it in an alembeck, keep the first water by itself, and so the second, and the third will be good vinegar, if afterwards you colour it with some of the berries. Distil it with a slow fire, and do not fill the still too full.

This water is excellent for the stomach.
Hannah Wolley, Queen-like Closet (1672).

HOW TO MAKE WINE-ROYAL OF ELDERBERRIES

To every gallon of fair water take four pounds of Malaga raisins picked from the stalks and shred, put them together in an open vessel with a taphole, stir them well together, and let them stand two or three days, then draw off all the clear liquor by the tap, and press out the rest strongly, put both

52

your liquors together, and to every gallon of it put a pint of the juice of elderberries, put them together in a clean dry cask well perfumed, keep open the bunghole that it may work; let it stand a fortnight, then rack it off the gross lee into another clean dry cask well perfumed, let it not be full by a gallon, stop it up close, leaving only a peg hole open or loose stopped; when you perceive it has done working, and that it has left off hissing, and is quiet, fill it up, and stop it very close and in two or three months' time it will be fit to drink.

The Family Physitian (1696).

VINUM SAMBUCEUM; OR WINE OF ELDERBERRIES

Take elderberries, when pretty ripe, plucked from the green stalks, what quantity you please, and press them that the juice may freely run from them, which may be done in a cider-press, or between two weighty planks, or for want of this opportunity you may mash them, and then it will run easily; this juice put up in a well-seasoned cask, and to every barrel put three gallons of water strong of honey boiled in it, and add some ale yeast to make it ferment, and work out the grossness of its body; then to clarify it add flour, whites of eggs and a little fixed nitre, and when it has well fermented, and grows fine, draw it from the settlings, and keep it till spring, then to every barrel add five pounds of its own flower, and as much loaf sugar, and then let it stand seven days, at the end whereof it will grow very rich, and have a curious flavour.

Its virtues. It is an excellent febrifuge, cleanses the blood of acidity, venom and putrefaction, good in measles, small-pox, swine-pox, and pestilential diseases; it contributes to rest and takes away the heat that afflicts the brain, easing pains in the head.

The Way to get Wealth (1706).

RED OR WHITE ELDER WINE

Gather the elderberries ripe and dry, pick them and bruise them with your hands, and strain them, then set the liquor by in glazed earthen vessels, for twelve hours to settle; then put to every pint of juice, a pint and half of water, and to every gallon of this liquor put three pounds of Lisbon sugar; set this in a kettle over the fire, and when it is ready to boil, clarify it with the whites of four or five eggs, let it boil an hour, and when it is almost cold, work it with strong ale yeast, and then turn it, filling up the vessel from time to time with the same liquor, saved on purpose, as it sinks by working. In a month's time, if the vessel holds about eight gallons, it will be fine and fit to bottle, and after bottling, will be fit to drink in two months; but remember all liquors must be fine before they are bottled, or else they will grow sharp and ferment in the bottles, and never be good for anything.

N.B.—Add to every gallon of this liquor, a pint of strong mountain wine, but not such as has the *borachio*, or hogskin flavour. This wine will be very strong and pleasant, and will keep good for several years.

We must prepare our red elder wine in the same manner as that we make with sugar, and if the vessel holds about eight or ten gallons, it will be fit for bottling in about a month's time, but if the vessel be larger, it must stand longer in proportion, three or four months at least for a hogshead.

The British Jewel (1782).

TO MAKE ELDER-FLOWER WINE

To twelve gallons of water put thirty pounds of single loaf sugar, boil it till two gallons be wasted, scum it well, let it stand till it is as cool as wort, then put in two quarts of blossoms picked from the stalks, stirring it every day till it has done working, which will not be under five or six days, then strain it and put it into the vessel; after it is stopped down, let it stand two months, and then, if fine, bottle it.

The British Jewel (1782).

TO MAKE RAISIN ELDER WINE

Take six gallons of water, and boil it half an hour, and when it has boiled, add to every gallon of water, five pounds of Malaga raisins, shred small; pour the water boiling hot upon them, and let it stand nine days, stirring it twice a day; boil your elder-berries as you do currants for jelly, and strain it all very fine; then add to every gallon of liquor, a pint of elderberry juice. When you have stirred all well together, spread a round of bread, half an inch thick, of a quartern loaf toasted on both sides, with yeast, put this into it, and let it work a day and a night, then put it in a vessel, which be sure to fill as it works over; when it has done working, stop it up for five or six months, and then it will be fine and fit to bottle.

Daily Companion (1799).

ELDER WINE

Strip the elderberries clean from the stalks; to every quart when well bruised put a quart of water. Boil it well ¾ of an hour then strain it off. To every quart of liquor put one pound of moist sugar, with some cinnamon, cloves, and a small pinch of hops. Boil it well ½ an hour. When cool work it with yeast. Barrel it next day—when the fermentation ceases add some brandy. Cork it down close and in six months bottle it.

Mrs. Tucker's Recipe. MS. Book of Recipes G24 (early nineteenth century).

TO MAKE RED ELDER WINE

Take 20 lb. of Malaga raisins, shred very small, then take 5 gallons of water, pour it on them boiling hot after the water has boiled an hour, then let it stand 10 days, stirring it every day. Strain it through a hair-sieve, having in readiness 6 pints of elderberry juice, thus taken—put the berries into a convenient earthen pot close stopped, and set them into boiling water and as the juice rises take it off and put it cold into the liquor then stir them well together, afterwards turn it into a vessel which must be full, let it stand in a warm place two months and if it is fine, bottle it.

MS. Book of Recipes B62 (early nineteenth century).

WHITE ELDER WINE

Take 6 gallons of river water well boiled and scummed, let it stand till it is better than blood warm, have ready 26 lb. of Malaga raisins chopped small. Pour the water upon them with the peels and juice of 6 large lemons and 4 oz. of elder flowers. Let it stand a fortnight in a deep tub close covered, stirring it every day. Squeeze the raisins with your hands, then strain it through a hair sieve into a suitable vessel, then put to it 2 lb. of loaf sugar, stirring it well to make it work and stop it up in 2 or 3 days. Let it stand 5 or 6 weeks before you bottle it, draw a quart of the wine and dissolve in it 2 oz. of isinglass beaten, put it into the vessel stirring it with a whisk, let it stand a fortnight at least before you bottle it. It will keep a year.

MS. Book of Recipes B62 (early nineteenth century).

TO MAKE ELDER WINE WITH CYDER

Boil or bake the berries, strain them through a sieve, boil the juice with the sugar, three pounds to every gallon. Add one quart of juice to every gallon of cyder, put the cyder and juice into a cask with a little ginger and Jamaica peppercorns. Stir it all together in the barrel—it will work without yeast. When it has done working stop it close.

N.B.—This is an excellent wine and will keep seven years. You may either bottle it the March following, or let it be drawn from the cask. Do not forget to put a little brandy in the bottle when you draw it off.

MS. Book of Recipes A5 (1833).

ELDERBERRY WINE (VERY GOOD)

Strip the berries, which should be fresh, and gathered on a dry day, clean from the stalks, and measure them into a tub or large earthen pan. Pour boiling water on them, in the proportion of two gallons to three of berries, press them down into the liquor, cover them closely, and let them remain until the following day; then strain the juice from the fruit through a sieve or cloth, and, when this is done, squeeze from the berries the greater part of the remaining juice, mix it with that which was first poured off, measure the whole, add to it three pounds of sugar, three quarters of an ounce of cloves, and one ounce of ginger, for every gallon, and boil it twenty minutes, keeping it thoroughly skimmed. Put it, when something more than milk-warm, into a perfectly dry and sweet cask (or if but a very very small quantity of wine be made, into large stone bottles, which answer the purpose quite well), fill this entirely, and set the wine directly, with a large spoonful of new yeast dropped into the bung-hole and stirred round in the liquor, or with a small toasted crust thickly spread with yeast.

In from fourteen to twenty days this wine will have fermented sufficiently; in three months it will be ready to drink; but it is better, and more wholesome, when longer kept.

Mrs. Acton (1854).

FIGS

Figs are usually classed into two main categories, according to their shape, either roundish or elongated, pear-like. In each of the two groups there are figs with deep purple skins and others with pale green skin or else green tinged with brown. At present figs are mostly cultivated under glass, in England, although they ripen in the open in some sheltered corners of walled gardens as far north as Scotland, and in less favoured positions in the West of England. There must have been a time, however, when figs grew much more freely than they do now in this country, since there appear to have been sufficient quantities of them to use in the making of wine.

WINE OF ENGLISH FIGS

To do this, take large blue figs, pretty ripe, steep them in white wine, having made some slits in them that they may swell, and gather in the substance of the wine, then slice some other figs, and let them simmer over a fire in fair water till they are reduced to a kind of pulp, strain out the water, pressing the pulp hard, and pour it as hot as may be to those figs that are infused in the wine; let the quantities be near equal, the water somewhat more than the wine and figs; then having infused twenty-four hours, mash them well together, and draw off what will run voluntarily, then press the rest, and if it proved not pretty sweet, add loaf sugar to render it so; let it ferment, and add a little honey, and sugar-candy to it, then fine it with whites of eggs and a little isinglass and so draw it off, and keep it for use.

Its Virtues. This is chiefly appropriated to defects of the lungs, helping shortness of breath, removing colds or inflammations of the lungs; it also comforts the stomach, and eases pains of the bowels.

The Way to get Wealth (1706).

GILLIFLOWER

This is the name, or one of the names, by which the old-fashioned clove carnations were known : other names were clove pink and picotees. Deep purple in colour, they possess a spicy scent not unlike that of cloves, and they were used extensively, in olden times, to flavour not only wines and cordials but sauces, soups and stews.

GILLIFLOWER WINE

To three gallons of water, put six pounds of the best powdered sugar; boil the sugar and water together for the space of half

57

an hour, keep scumming it as the scum rises, let it stand to cool; beat up three ounces of the syrup of betony, with a large spoonful of ale yeast, put it into the liquor and brew it well together; then having a peck of gilliflowers cut from the stalks, put them into the liquor, let them infuse and work together three days, covered with a cloth, strain it and put it into a cask, let it settle for three or four weeks, then bottle it.

The British Jewel (1782).

GINGER

Ginger is the dried rhizome (root-stock and underground stem) of an East India plant, which is now cultivated in many parts of the world. Black ginger and white ginger are merely the unpeeled and peeled varieties of the same root. Ginger has a pleasant, somewhat peppery taste of its own, and it is supposed to possess a stimulating action upon the digestive organs and the circulation of the blood.

GINGER WINE

Take fourteen quarts of water, and one ounce of rance ginger sliced, with three pounds of sugar; boil them over a clear fire for half an hour, then take them off; and when the liquor is new-milk warm, put into it three lemons, with a little good yeast; close up the vessel and let it stand five days. If it be wrought clear in that time, you may bottle it. If not, let it stand longer, until it be well wrought, and in ten days after you may drink it.

The Practical Distiller (1734).

MRS. BROWN'S RECEIPT FOR GINGER WINE

Two ounces of ginger to a gallon of water made pretty warm. Let it stand all night. Strain it off in the morning then slice the ginger and put it in the water again with 2¾ lb. soft sugar and the peel of a large lemon boiled in it. Let it boil an hour or rather better and skim it well then strain it off and let it stand till it is cold, then squeeze the juice of the lemon and then work it as you do any other wine.

MS. Recipes Book F2 (1805)

TO MAKE GINGER WINE

To 6 gallons of water put 6 lb. of fine Lisbon sugar, 5 oz. ginger cut in small pieces, the thin parings of 12 lemons. Let all boil for half an hour. Let it stand until milk-warm, then add 6 tablespoonfuls of barm. Squeeze the juice of the lemons into the wine, pour some water on the lemons and let them stand, just cover them all night. Then pour the clear water from them into the whole. Coarsely chop 2½ lb. raisins into it. Stir it once a day for nine days, then add a quart of brandy. Well stop it up and it will be fit for use in 6 months.

MS. Book of Recipes (1820).

GINGER BEER

To 10 gallons of water put 12 lb. of lump sugar, 12 lemons, and 8 oz. of best ginger. Boil the sugar in the water, and when the scum has done rising, add the ginger and lemon peels; boil ½ hour; when new-milk warm, put in the juice of the lemons, and as much yeast as will ferment it in the tub a day or two. Then put it all in a barrel, and in a month it will be ready.

MS. Book of Recipes D3 (1727).

GINGER BEER

14 gallons of water	14 lemons, rind and juice.
14 lb. of sugar	5 whites of eggs
14 oz. of ginger	2 tablespoonfuls of ale yeast

All the water must be boiled. Put the eggs and sugar in first with the water. When quite free from scum add the ginger sliced thin, or bruised, and boil one hour. Strain the juice of the lemons through muslin, the rind cut very thin. Put both into the cask and when the liquor is quite cold pour it on the rind and juice, last of all the yeast. Bung it tight and let it stand a fortnight, then bottle and in another fortnight it is fit for use. When boiled, the ginger is to be kept back.

MS. Book of Recipes E3 (1820).

GOLDEN CORDIAL

Take one gallon of the best French brandy; add to it two ounces of spirit of saffron, two drachms of the confection of *Alkermes*, and one drachm of the oil of cloves; one pound of double refined sugar, one grain of musk, and one grain of amber grease.

Mix the confection of *Alkermes* in a marble or glass mortar with a little of the said brandy; and incorporate your oil of cloves with the loaf sugar, by dropping it thereon, and grinding them together; then put the brandy into a wide-mouthed bottle, with the rest of the ingredients; shake them well together, and close the mouth of the glass over with a wet bladder and leather, shaking the bottle every day. Then let the liquor settle, and strain it through a jelly-bag; when it hath stood some time, decant off the clear liquor, and into every quart put three leaves of gold.

If the colour be not high enough it may be augmented by hanging in the glass a little saffron tied up in a bag, which will bring it to due perfection, viz., of a beautiful gold colour; and in case of necessity, the same may well supply the place of its spirit, where it is not easily to be had, by adding a due proportion; as about three drachms will suffice to impregnate the whole quantity prescribed.

It is a very rich cordial, both in price and goodness. It wonderfully refreshes the spirits, and invigorates the whole nervous system; and may very profitably be used in all languors, faintness, and sinking of the spirits, whether proceeding from a hysterical, or other disorder; especially where the perfumes are not offensive. For some persons cannot bear their smell or taste without great prejudice; and therefore this and the like perfumed cordials are always to be avoided by them, unless they would run the hazard of fainting.

The Practical Distiller (1734).

GOLDEN CORDIAL

For two gallons, take two gallons of malt spirit, two drams and a half of double perfumed *Alkermes*, one quarter of a dram of oil of cloves, one ounce of spirit of saffron, three pounds of loaf sugar, powdered, and one book of leaf gold.

N.B.—First put your brandy in a large bottle, then put three or four spoonfuls of it into a small cup; mix your *Alkermes* in it and then put in your oil of cloves, and mix that; do the like with the spirit of saffron, and pour all into the bottle of brandy. Afterwards put in your sugar, then cork your bottle, and tie or wire the cork. Shake it well together frequently for three or four days, and let it stand for a fortnight. You must set the bottle so that, when racked off into other bottles, it will only be gently tilted. Put into every bottle, two leaves of gold, cut small. You may put two quarts of spirits to the dregs, and it will make a good cordial, though inferior to the first.

ANOTHER WAY

One gallon of brandy or spirits, two pounds of loaf sugar, one dram of confection *Alkermes,* one dram of the oil of cloves, and one ounce of spirit of saffron.

N.B.—Powder your sugar, and mix it in your brandy; then put in the rest, and stir it all one way for a quarter of an hour.

J. Davies (1811).

GOLDEN WATER

To a quart of spirits of wine, add twelve drops of oil of aniseed, six drops of oil of cinnamon, eight of oil of citron, and three drops of oil of roses; as soon as the oils are dissolved, mix with it a quart of the syrup; filter it and before you bottle the liquor, stir into it a square of leaf-gold cut into very little bits; if silver leaf is added instead, it goes by the name of silver water.

Indian Domestic Economy (1849).

GOOSEBERRIES

The gooseberry is a native of Europe and North Africa. It was introduced in England in the sixteenth century, and many varieties have been cultivated and improved since then in all parts of the British Isles. Gooseberries differ as regards shape and skin. In shape, they belong either to the round or to the oval category. In each of those two categories there are varieties with smooth and downy or rough and hairy skin, which may be either red, yellow, green or white, when the fruit is ripe. Unlike most other fruits, gooseberries must be picked before they are ripe if they are to be used for making any sort of wine or cordial. They have long been among the prime favourites in cottage gardens and used for home-made wines to a larger extent than most other fruits.

TO MAKE ROYAL-WINE OF GOOSEBERRIES, OR CURRANTS, WITHOUT SPIRITS OR SUGAR

If you will make wine-royal, either of currants or gooseberries, without sugar and spirits, then to every gallon of liquor put two pounds of Malaga raisins shred, stir it well together, and let it stand four-and-twenty hours; then press it out, and strain it and put the liquor into a cask, and after a fortnight rack it off from the gross lees into another clean dry cask; stop it close, leaving only a little peg or fasset hole open, or the peg loosely in it, till you perceive it has left off hissing, and is quiet, then fill up your cask with the same liquor, and so keep it full till you bottle it.

You may also put your raisins, being shred, amongst your currants or gooseberries broken to pieces, and liquor, and in four-and-twenty hours after press it out; and thus you make but one pressing.

The Family Physician (1696).

WINE OF GOOSEBERRIES

A curious cooling wine may be made of gooseberries, after the following directions.

Take gooseberries just beginning to turn to ripeness, but not those that are ripe, bruise them well, as you did the grapes, but not so as to break their seeds, then pour to every eight pounds of pulp a gallon of clear spring-water, or rather their own distilled water, made in a cold still, and let them stand in the vessel covered in a cool place twenty-four hours, then put them into a strong canvas or hair bag, and press out all the juice that will run from them, and to every quart of it put twelve ounces of loaf, or other fine sugar, stirring it till it be thoroughly melted. Then put it up into a well-seasoned cask, and set it in a cool place, for too much heat will sour it, and when it has purged, and settled about twenty or thirty days, fill the vessel full, and bung it down close, that as little air as possible may come at it.

When you find it is well wrought and settled, then is your time to draw it off into smaller casks or bottles, keeping them also in cool places, for there is nothing more that damages any sorts of wines than heat.

And as the wine of grapes has many virtues, in comforting and strengthening the heart, reviving and restoring the faded spirits, so this has not a few proper to it, conducing to the health of man.

Its Virtue. This is a curious cooling drink, taken with great success in all hot diseases, as fevers, small-pox, the hot fit of the ague; it stops laxation, and is good in the bloody-flux, cools the heat of the liver and stomach, stops bleeding, and mitigates inflammations; it wonderfully abates the flushing and redness of the face after hard drinking, or the like; it provokes

urine, and is good against the stone, but those that are of a very phlegmatic constitution, it is not so proper for them.
The Way to get Wealth (1706).

PEARL GOOSEBERRY WINE

Take as many as you please of the best pearl gooseberries, bruise them, and let them stand all night, the next morning press or squeeze them out, and let the liquor stand to settle seven or eight hours; then pour off the clear from the settling, and measure it as you put it into your vessel, adding to every three pints of liquor a pound of double-refined sugar; break your sugar in small lumps, and put it in the vessel, with a bit of isinglass, stop it up, and at three months' end bottle it off, putting into every bottle a lump of double refined sugar. This is the fine gooseberry wine.
Gelleroy—London Cook (1762).

TO MAKE GOOSEBERRY WINE

Gather your gooseberries in dry weather, when they are half ripe, pick them and bruise them in a tub with a wooden mallet, or such-like instrument, for no metal is proper; then take about the quantity of a peck of the gooseberries, put them into a cloth made of horse-hair, and press them as much as possible, without breaking the seeds; repeat this work till all your gooseberries are pressed, adding to this pressed juice, the other which you will find in the tub; than add to every gallon three pounds of powdered sugar (for Lisbon sugar will give the wine a taste which may be disagreeable to some people), and besides it will sweeten much more than dry powder; stir it together until all the sugar is dissolved, and then put it in a vessel or cask, which must be quite filled with it. If the vessel holds about ten or twelve gallons it must stand a fortnight or three weeks, or if about twenty gallons, then about four or five weeks, to settle, in a cool place; then draw off the wine from the lees, return the clear liquor into the vessel again, and let it stand three months, if the cask is about three gallons, or between four or five months if it be twenty gallons, and then bottle it off. We must note that a small cask of any liquor is sooner ripe and fit for drinking, than the liquor of a large cask must be; but a small body of liquor will sooner change sour than that which is the largest cask. The wine, if it is truly prepared, according to the above directions, will improve every year, and keep several years.

The British Jewel (1782).

RED GOOSEBERRY WINE

Take thirty-six pounds of red gooseberries, when they are full ripe, and begin to drop off the trees; bruise them, and pour upon them twelve quarts of boiling water; let them stand twenty-four hours; then strain it through a flannel bag, and add to the liquor twelve pounds of good Lisbon sugar; stir it well together, and the next day put it into the vessel, and in four months bottle it.

N.B.—It is best when kept to three or four years old.

Addison Ashburn (1807).

GREEN GOOSEBERRY WINE

To every pound of gooseberries when picked and bruised put one quart of water. Let it stand three days, stirring it twice a day. To every gallon of juice when strained, put three and a half pounds of loaf sugar. Barrel it directly, and to every twenty gallons of liquor add a quart of brandy, and hang a bit of isinglass in the vessel—keep it a year in the barrel, unless you find by plugging the sweetness goes off, then bottle it sooner.

The gooseberries to be full grown, but not turned.

MS. Book of Recipes G14 (early nineteenth century).

BRISK GOOSEBERRY WINE

Let forty pounds of unripe gooseberries be mashed, and having poured upon the mass one gallon of water, squeeze out the juice, add to it twelve pounds of lump sugar, and six ounces of super-tartrate of potash, previously reduced to a fine powder, suffer the liquor to ferment in a tub for about two days only, and then transfer it into a cask, and attend to the process of replenishing the waste liquor by filling up the cask from time to time, till the fermentation has so far subsided that the hissing noise which is heard at the bung-hole is but slightly perceptible. The bung of the cask may then be fastened down, and also the spile, and the cask left undisturbed in a cool cellar, till the month of November, at which time the clear liquor should be racked off into a cask and bottled.

The New London Cookery (c. 1827).

EFFERVESCING GOOSEBERRY WINE

Ingredients.—To every gallon of water allow 6 lb. of green gooseberries and 3 lb. of lump sugar.

Mode.—This wine should be prepared from unripe gooseberries, in order to avoid the flavour which the fruit would give to the wine when in a mature state. Its briskness depends more upon the time of bottling than upon the unripe state of the fruit, for effervescing wine can be made from fruit that is ripe as well as that which is unripe. The fruit should be selected when it has nearly attained its full growth, and consequently before it shows any tendency to ripen. Any bruised or decayed berries, and those that are very small, should be rejected. The blossom and stalk ends should be removed, and the fruit well bruised in a tub or pan, in such quantities as to insure each berry being broken without crushing the seeds. Pour the water (which should be warm) on the fruit, squeeze and stir it with the hand until all the pulp is removed from the skin and seeds, and cover the whole closely for 24 hours; after which strain it through a coarse bag, and press it with as much force as can be conveniently applied, to extract the whole of the juice and liquor the fruit may contain. To every 40 or 50 lb. of fruit one gallon more of hot water may be passed through the *mare*, or husks, in order to obtain any soluble matter that may remain, and be again pressed. The juice should be put into a tub or pan of sufficient size to contain all of it, and the sugar added to it. Let it be well stirred until the sugar is dissolved, and place the pan in a warm situation; keep it closely covered, and let it ferment for a day or two. It must then be drawn off into clean casks, placed a little on one side for the scum that arises to be thrown out, and the casks kept filled with the remaining "must" that should be reserved for that purpose. When the active fermentation has ceased, the casks should be plugged upright, again filled if necessary, the bungs be put in loosely and, after a few days, when the fermentation is a little more languid (which may be known by the hissing noise ceasing), the bungs should be driven in tight, and a spile-hole made, to give vent if necessary. About November or December, on a clear fine day, the wine should be racked from its lees into clean casks, which may be rinsed with brandy. After a month it should be examined to see if it is sufficiently clear for bottling; if not, it must be fined with isinglass, which may be dissolved in some of the wine : 1 oz. will be sufficient for 9 gallons. In March or April, or when the gooseberry bushes begin to blossom, the wine must be bottled, in order to insure its being effervescing.

Seasonable. Make this the end of May or beginning of June, before the berries ripen.

Mrs. Beeton (1861).

TO MAKE GOOSEBERRY VINEGAR

To 3 quarts of water, 1 quart of gooseberries, and in that proportion for as great a quantity as you please. Boil the water, and let it stand till it is almost cold. Bruise the gooseberries and put them into the water, and let it stand 24 hours, then strain it through a flannel bag, and to every gallon you make, put a pound of the coarsest sugar. As soon as that is dissolved put it into the vessel. Stop it up with brown paper pricked full of holes, let it stand in a garret or cellar a year—by then bottle it. Gooseberries must be ripe.

MS. Book of Recipes E1 (early nineteenth century).

GOUT CORDIAL

Raisins 12 ounces, stoned and chopped small.
Senna ½ ounce; Saffron ¼ ounce;
Fennel Seed ¼ ounce; Rhubarb 2 ounces;
Cochineal ¼ ounce; Coriander ¼ ounce;
Cardamum ¼ ounce.

Infuse 2 drachms of liquorice with the above ingredients in two quarts of the best brandy; let it stand ten days in a warm place, shaking it every day; strain it off, and put one quart more of brandy on the ingredients.

A glass of this may be taken when the pain is very bad; and if not better an hour after, half a glass, or a third of a glass more will do in general.

GRAPES

TO MAKE WINE OF ENGLISH GRAPES, TO BE AS STRONG, WHOLESOME AND PLEASING AS FRENCH WINE

When you perceive your grapes to be plump and transparent, and the seeds or stones to come forth black and clear, and not clammy, and the stalks begin to wither then gather them, the weather being dry for some time before. Cut them off from the branches and not pull them, and in the moon's decrease, preserving them from bruises as much as you can; then cut the stalks as close to the clusters as you can, before you press out your wine.

To every gallon of juice or must take two pounds of the best Malaga raisins picked from the stalks, and shred, put them together in a vat, the head being out, and let there be a tap at the bottom with a taphole, as in a meshtub; stir your liquor and raisins well together and let them stand twenty-four hours: then draw off all the liquor by the tap that will run, and press out the raisins as strong as you can, then put both liquors together in a cask, which must be full, and leave the bunghole open, that it may work and cast out any foulness; after ten, twelve, or fourteen days, draw it off from the lees into a clean and dry cask, which must not be full, but leave a part of the vessel void or empty, stop it up close immediately, and that very well, lest it loose its spirits, which vacancy you may again supply when it hath done working with other liquor or wine of the same that has also fermented in any other vessel. After you have thus closed up your bung, you ought to leave open the small venthole or fassethole, only loosely putting in the peg or fasset, lest otherwise the wild spirits that are in the liquor force a passage; which by the easy stopping this vent and sometimes opening it may be prevented until you find it hath wasted that wild spirit.

The Family Physitian (1696).

TO MAKE GRAPE WINE

Put a gallon of water to a gallon of grapes, bruise the grapes well, let them stand a week without stirring, and then draw off the liquor; put to a gallon of the wine, three pounds of sugar, and then put it into a vessel, but do not fasten it up with your bung till it has done hissing, let it stand two months, and it will draw clear and fine; if you think proper, you may then bottle it, but remember your cork is quite close, and keep it in a good dry cellar.

The Daily Companion (1799).

GRAPE WINE

To one gallon of grapes put one gallon of water; bruise the grapes, let them stand a week without stirring, then draw off

and fine. Put to a gallon of wine three pounds of sugar, put it in a vessel; but it must not be stopped till it has done hissing.
Bishop (1860).

HAWTHORN WINE

Pour 1 gallon of water on 4 double handfuls of hawthorn flowers. Let it stand 2 days. Strain liquor off, boil and pour again on same flowers. Let it stand 2 more days. Again strain and add 3 lb. moist sugar to the gallon and boil together 20 minutes. Put back in pansion (? pancheon—it is a large earthenware vessel with wide open top : it was the local name in Notts) with piece of toast with 1 tablespoon of yeast on it to the gallon. Let stand one day, then put in barrel, and let it be till it has done working (about a fortnight or more), then lightly bung barrel and bottle in 3 or 4 months.
From Lady Barker's grandmother's MS. recipe book.

HEART'S-EASE

The name of the little wild pansy with five petals, purple, white and yellow. It was recommended in olden times as a remedy for asthma and it also had the reputation of being a love charm, hence one of its many country names is Love-in-Idleness.

HEART'S-EASE WATER

Take what quantity you please of *Aquavitæ* or artificial brandy, and to every gallon put a pound of seeds of heart's-ease, and the like quantity of the blossoms, well dried in the sun; tie them up in a bag, put them into the still, and draw as long as you find any pleasant taste in the spirit; then sweeten it with the syrup made of heart's-ease and white sugar; put it up in a cask, adding to it two or three spoonfuls of new yeast, and the white of an egg or two, beaten up with flour, whereby it will have its fermentation, and be refined fit for sale; being a very pleasant water.

Now, observe, in the distillation of this, there will be apt to come over it an oil, or white thick spirit; this to be fined as it comes, take a fine Holland cloth, and rub it very well on one side with black lead, and bind the side so rubbed inwards, towards the end of the worm, and so the thickness will be kept

68

back. And thus other waters, of the like nature, may be ordered, and prepared for sale, or private use.

The Way to get Wealth (1706).

HIPPOCRAS
ENGLISH HYPOCRAS
Infuse for a few hours in about three quarts of white wine one pound and a half of loaf sugar, an ounce of cinnamon, two or three tops of sweet marjoram, and a little long pepper all beaten in a mortar. Run the liquor through a filtering bag, with a grain of musk, and add thereto the juice of a large lemon; warm it moderately over the fire, pour it again on the spicery, and when it has stood three or four days, strain it off, and bottle it for use. If wanted to be red, port wine may be used, or the liquor coloured with the juice of elder or mulberries, cochineal, etc.

The New London Cookery (1827).

HIPPOCRAS
Take one ounce of cinnamon, two drachms of ginger, two pennyweights of cloves, nutmeg, and galingal, a pennyweight of each. Pound these together well, and infuse them in a pint of red or white wine, and a pint of malmsey; to this add a pound of the best loaf sugar. These proportions will make a quart of the liquor.

Bishop (1860).

HUNGARY WATER
Take seven pounds of the tops of rosemary with the leaves and flowers, six gallons of rectified spirits, and two quarts of water, and distil off five gallons with a moderate fire.

The New London Cookery (c. 1827).

IMPERIAL NECTAR
For three gallons, take six quarts of malt spirit, two quarts of raisin wine, two ounces of peach and apricot kernels, one pennyweight of oil of orange, half a pennyweight of the oil of cloves, a quarter of an ounce of mace, two large nutmegs, half a pint of spirit of wine, and two pounds of loaf sugar. Fill up with water.

N.B.—The kernels, mace and nutmegs must be bruised in a mortar and steeped in some spirits for eight or ten days. Colour it with burnt sugar, of a fair brown colour, and let it stand to fine itself.

ANOTHER WAY

For three gallons, peel eighteen lemons very thin, and steep the peelings for forty-eight hours in a gallon of brandy; then add the juice, with five quarts of spring water, three pounds of loaf sugar, and two nutmegs grated; stir it till the sugar is dissolved; then pour in three quarts of new milk, boiling hot, and let it stand two hours, after which run it through a jelly bag, till fine. This is fit for immediate use, but may be kept for years in bottles, and will be improved by age.

J. Davies (1811).

LEMON

The lemon, which is the fruit of the lemon tree, the most valuable of the citrus species, not even excepting the orange tree, is rich in citric acid and oil of lemon, the first being in the juice of the fruit and the other in its rind. Both have been and still are used extensively in the making of all kinds of refreshing beverages, whether alcoholic or not.

TO MAKE LEMON WATER

Take twelve of the fairest lemons, slice them, and put them into two pints of white wine, and put to them of cinnamon and galingale, of each one quarter of an ounce, of red rose leaves, burrage and bugloss flowers, of each one handful, of yellow sanders one dram, steep all these together 12 hours, then distil them gently in a glass still, put into the glass where it drops three ounces of sugar, and one grain of ambergris.

Queen-like Closet, Hannah Wolley (1672).

LEMON WATER

Take the peels (very thinly pared) of three large lemons; infuse them in three pints of brandy for five or six days, and then strain off the liquor.

In the mean time take a quart of spring water, and ten ounces of double-refined sugar; boil them up to a thin syrup, scum it clear, and then put in a little cinnamon, with two or three cloves, one large blade of mace, and a little nutmeg; boil these a little longer, until they have given it a fine flavour; then take the liquor from the fire, and let it stand until it be cold: and if there be any scum or dross upon it, strain it whilst hot through a jelly-bag. Mix both these liquors together when the former is fully cold, and bottle the mixture.

This is a pleasant cordial water, of an easy composition, and a moderate price, and much preferable in my opinion, to the made wine going under the same title. It may be used in all cases where a cordial dram is required, and is a pretty closet medicine. After the same manner may be prepared an orange water, which will be found no less stomachic than the other, and as grateful to the palate in all respects.

The Practical Distiller (1734).

TO MAKE LEMON WINE

Pare off the rinds of six large lemons, cut them and squeeze out the juice, steep the rinds in the juice, and put to it a quart of brandy, let stand three days in an earthen pot close stopped; then squeeze six more, and mix it with two quarts of spring water, and as much sugar as will sweeten the whole; boil the water, lemons and sugar together, and let it stand till it is cool; then add a quart of white wine, mix them together, and run it through a flannel bag into some vessel where your brandy is; let it stand three months, and then bottle it off, cork your bottles well, and take care to keep them cool, and it will be fit to drink in a month or six weeks.

Lemon wine may be made to drink like citron water, the method of which is as follows; pare fine a dozen of lemons very thin, put the peels into five quarts of French brandy, and let them stand fourteen days; then make the juice into a syrup with three pounds of single refined sugar, and when the peels are ready, boil fifteen gallons of water, with forty pounds of single refined sugar, for half an hour; then put it into a tub and when cool, add to it one spoonful of barm, and let it work two days; then turn it, and put it in the brandy, peels and syrup, stir them all together, and close up your cask, let it stand three months, then bottle it, and it will be as pale as any citron water.

Daily Companion (1799?).

71

LEMONADE

Take 1 quart of brandy, the yellow rinds of 12 lemons cut very thin, steep them in the brandy 4 or 5 days, then put in 1 quart Rhenish or small pale white wine, take out the peels and put in with the wine the juice of 12 lemons, and sweeten it to your taste with the best double-refined sugar, let it run through a jelly-bag but not squeeze it. Bottle it and when it has stood 4 or 5 days, clear it off into other bottles. The longer it is kept the better it will drink.

MS. Book of Recipes (early nineteenth century).

EXCELLENT PORTABLE LEMONADE

Rasp, with a quarter-pound of sugar, the rind of a very fine juicy lemon, reduce it to powder, and pour on it the strained juice of the fruit. Press the mixture into a jar, and when wanted for use dissolve a tablespoonful of it in a glass of water. It will keep a considerable time. If too sweet for the taste of the drinker, a very small portion of citric acid may be added when it is taken.

Mrs. Acton (1854).

DELICIOUS MILK LEMONADE

Dissolve six ounces of loaf sugar in a pint of boiling water, and mix with them a quarter-pint of lemon-juice, and the same quantity of sherry, then add three-quarters of a pint of cold milk, stir the whole well together, and pass it through a jelly-bag till clear.

Mrs. Acton (1854).

MACARONI CORDIAL

Infuse for a fortnight in nine pints of brandy, a pound of bitter almonds, with a little Bohemian or Spanish angelica-root beaten together, shaking the vessel often. At the end of that time, put the whole into a cucurbite, and distil it in a water bath. Five pints of spirit, thus impregnated with the flavour of the almonds and angelica, make a syrup with five pounds of sugar, two quarts of *eau-de-mille-fleurs*, and three quarts of common distilled water. When this is mixed with the spirits, add thirty drops of the essence of lemons, after which, filter it through blotting paper.

The New London Cookery (c. 1827).

MALT WINE

Ingredients.—5 gallons of water, 28 lb. of sugar, 6 quarts of sweet-wort, 6 quarts of tun, 3 lb. of raisins, ½ lb. of candy, 1 pint of brandy.

Mode.—Boil the sugar and water together for 10 minutes; skim it well, and put the liquor into a convenient-sized pan or tub. Allow it to cool; then mix it with the sweet-wort and tun. Let it stand for 3 days, then put it into a barrel; here it will work or ferment for another three days or more; then bung up the cask, and keep it undisturbed for 2 or 3 months. After this, add the raisins (whole), the candy and brandy, and, in 6 months' time, bottle the wine off. Those who do not brew, may procure the sweet-wort and tun from any brewer. Sweet-wort is the liquor that leaves the mash of malt before it is boiled with the hops; tun is the new beer after the whole of the brewing operation has been completed.

Time.—To be boiled 10 minutes; to stand 3 days after mixing; to ferment 3 days; to remain in the cask 2 months before the raisins are added; bottle 6 months after.

Seasonable.—Make this in March or October.

Mrs. Beeton (1861).

MARIGOLD

Marigolds have been grown in cottage gardens in every part of the British Isles for hundreds of years, and they are still among the greatest favourites. And so they deserve to be, being easy to grow, cheerful to look at, and more helpful than a chemist's stock, if only they possess half the curing properties which the old herbals give them credit for.

MARIGOLD WINE

Boil 3½ lb. of lump sugar in a gallon of water, put in a gallon of marigold flowers, gathered dry and picked from the stalks, and make it as directed for cowslip wine. If the flowers are gathered only a few at a time, measure them when they are picked, turn and dry them in the shade; and when there is a sufficient quantity, put them into the barrel, and pour the sugar and water upon them. Put a little brandy into the bottles when it is bottled off.

The New Female Instructor.

73

RECEIPT FOR COWSLIP, OR MARIGOLD WINE

To every gallon of water take two pounds and a half of sugar, boil this an hour, and scum it well, and pour it, boiling hot, upon the yellow tops of either sorts of flowers. To every gallon of the liquor put half a peck of flowers nicely cut, let this steep all night, and to each gallon squeeze in two or three lemons, with a piece of peel cut thin. When these have steeped a night and a day, work it with toasted bread, as directed in elder wine, with yeast. When you put it in your vessel pour it from the settlement; and when it has worked as long as it will, pour into every gallon one pint of Rhenish or white wine; if it is fine in six months you may bottle it; this will drink at three or four years old. Either sort is a cordial, wholesome and pleasant.

Daily Companion (1799).

TO MAKE MARYGOLD WINE

Take 20 lb. Malaga raisins, 5 gallons of water and about 2 gallons of Marygold flowers. Let the flowers be picked, and the raisins picked and rubbed clean between cloths and shredded small. Then put the flowers and raisins together into an earthen pot or into a tub. Boil the water and put it hot on to them and cover it with a cloth and let it stand 3 or 4 days, stirring it once or twice a day.

Then let it run through a hair sieve (pressing it only with the hands). Tun it up and let it stand three weeks or a month and then bottle it up. Let your vessel be full.

MS. Book of Recipes (early nineteenth century).

THE MELANCHOLY WATER

Take of the flowers of gilliflowers, four handfuls, rosemary flowers three handfuls, damask rose leaves, burrage and bugloss flowers of each one handful, of balm leaves six handfuls, of marigold flowers one handful, of pinks six handfuls, of cinnamon grossly beaten half an ounce, two nutmegs beaten, aniseeds beaten one ounce, three penniworth of saffron; put them all into a pottle of sack, and let them stand two days, stirring them sometimes well together; then distil them in an ordinary still, and let it drop into a glass wherein there is two grains of musk, and eight ounces of white sugar candy, and some leaf gold; take of this water three times a week fasting, two spoonfuls at a time, and oftener if you find need; distil with soft fire; this is good for women in child-bed if they are faint.

Queen-like Closet, Hannah Wolley (1672).

MINTS

There are many different varieties of mint, all of them possessing in a more or less marked degree a distinctive fragrance of their own which is highly refreshing. The mint of mint sauce is the *Mentha rotundifolia* or *viridis*, the common mint which may be seen in every English cottage garden. It is also known as spearmint. The mint used in the making of Cordials and Liqueurs is a different kind, the *Mentha piperita*, or *Peppermint*, fields of which were cultivated until recently at and near Mitcham, in Surrey, for the making of *Crème de Menthe*.

TO MAKE SPIRIT OF MINTS

Take three pints of the best white wine, three handfuls of right spear mint picked clean from the stalks, let it steep in wine tight covered; in the morning, put it into a copper alembeck and draw it with a pretty quick fire; and when you have drawn it all, take all your water and add as much wine as before, and put to the water, and the same quantity of mint as before, let it steep two or three hours, then put all into your still, and draw it with a soft fire, put into your receiver a quantity of loaf sugar, and you will find it very excellent; you may distil it in an ordinary still if you please; but then it will not be so strong nor effectual.

Thus you may do with any other herbs whatsoever.

Queen-like Closet, Hannah Wolley (1672).

WINE OF MINT, BALM, AND OTHER HERBS

To come more briefly to a conclusion of this chapter, know that the wine of mint, balm, and other fragrant herbs, are best made after this manner, *viz.*:

First, distil the herb in the cold still, then add honey to it, and work as in scurvygrass, and then refine it, and work it down by a due proportion of its own syrup, and so the wine will become very fragrant, and continue the whole virtue of the herb : wormwood wine, wine of rue, carduus, and such strong physical herbs may be made by infusion, only in small white wines, cider, perry or the like, adding a little sweets to palliate them, that they may be more agreeable to the taste. That of black currants may be made as of other currants, and are very proper to be kept in all families.

Their virtues. They indifferently all of them resist pestilential airs, are good in agues, and cold diseases; prevent mother-fits and vapours, and ease pains in the joints and sinews, cleansing the blood, and are great hinderers of apoplexies, epilepsies, and the like; and the wines have not only the virtues of the herbs, but an addition to heat, strengthen and revive decaying nature.

The Way to get Wealth (1706).

PEPPERMINT WATER

Gather the mint when full grown, and before it seeds. Cut it in short lengths, put it into your still, and cover it in water. Make a good fire under it, and when it is near boiling, and the still begins to drop, if you find the fire too hot, draw some away, that the liquor may not boil over. The slower the still drops, the clearer and stronger will be the water. The next day bottle it off, and after it has stood two or three days, cork it close, and it will preserve its strength a considerable time.

Anthony Haselmore (1823).

PEPPERMINT

For 20 gallons, take 13 of rectified malt spirit, fifteen pennyweights of the oil of peppermint, twelve pounds of loaf sugar, one pint and a half of the spirit of wine; fill up with water, and fine it as you do gin. You may make any quantity you like by reducing or increasing the ingredients proportionally. In killing your oils and working it, proceed also in the same manner as for gin.

J. Davies (1811).

MINT JULEP

May be made with claret, madeira, etc., but the usual way is as follows. Put into a tumbler about a dozen sprigs of the tender shoots of mint; upon them put a tablespoonful of finely pounded sugar or syrup, with equal proportions of peach and common brandy, so as to fill it up nearly one third, and fill up the remainder with rasped or pounded ice; as the ice melts you drink it.

Indian Domestic Economy (1849).

MIXED FRUITS

The following method of making an excellent wine is copied from the Bath Society's paper, vol. XI:

"Take cherries, black currants, white currants, and raspberries, of each an equal quantity, though if the black currants preponderate the better. To four pounds of the mixed fruit, well bruised, put one gallon of water; let it steep three days and nights in an open vessel, frequently stirring up the mass; then strain it through a hair sieve; the remaining pulp press to dryness : put both liquids together, and in each gallon of the liquid put three pounds of sugar; let the whole stand again three days and nights, frequently stirring it up as before, after skimming off the top; then tun it into a cask, and let it remain open at the bung-hole whilst fermenting about two weeks; lastly to every nine gallons put one quart of good brandy, and then fasten down the bung; if it does not soon become fine, a solution of isinglass may be stirred into the wine."

The New London Cooker (c. 1827).

MULBERRIES

Mulberries are the fruit of the black mulberry tree, probably a native of Persia, but introduced in England at an early date. Mulberries were used to make a medicinal wine long ago, when they were reputed to cure chest troubles, and they have also been used in the compounding of cordials.

WINE OF MULBERRIES

Take mulberries when they are just changed from their redness to shining black, gather them in a dry day when the sun has taken off the dew, spread them thinly on a fine cloth on some floor or table for twenty-four hours, boil up a gallon of water to each gallon of juice you press out of these; scum the water well, and add a little cinnamon grossly bruised, put to every gallon six ounces of white sugar-candy finely beaten, scum and strain the water when it is taken off and settled, then put to it the juice of mulberries, and to every gallon of the mixture a pint of white or Rhenish wine; let them stand in a cask to purge and settle five or six days, then draw off the wine; and keep it cool.

Its virtues. This is a very rich cordial, it gives vigour to consumptive bodies, allays the heat of the blood, prevents qualms and pukings in women, makes the body soluble, helps digestion and eases distempers in the bowels.

The Way to get Wealth (1706).

MULBERRY WINE

Gather your mulberries when they are ripe, beat them in a mortar, and to every quart of berries put a quart of spring water. When you put them into the tub mix them well, and let them stand all night; then strain them through a sieve, and to every gallon of liquor, put three pounds of sugar : when your sugar is dissolved put it into your cask, into which (if an eight-gallon one) you must put a gill of finings. Care must be taken that the cask be not too full, nor bunged too close at first. Set it in a cold place, and when fine, bottle it.

J. Davies (1811).

MULBERRY WINE

Take mulberries that are quite ripe; gather them when the weather is fine, spread them on a cloth on the floor or table for twenty-four hours, and boil up a gallon of water to a gallon of juice; skim the water well, and add a little cinnamon bruised. Add to every gallon six ounces of white sugar-candy, finely beaten, skim and strain the water when it is taken off and settled, and put to it the juice of the mulberries, and to every gallon of the mixture put a pint of white or Rhenish wine; let them stand six days in a cask to settle, then draw off the wine, and keep it cool. This is a very rich wine.

Bishop (1860).

MUM

Mum, according to the author's way, is thus : A vessel containing 6 gallons of water, boil it to the consumption of the third part, then let it be brewed with 7 bushels of ground beans, and when it is turned let not the hogshead be filled too full at first, and beginning to work put to it the inner rinds of fir-tree, three pounds of birch, and the leaves and tops of fir-tree each one pound, *Carduus Benedictus* dried three good handfuls : Burnet, betony, rosemary, marjoram, avens, pennyroyal, elder-flowers, wild thyme, of each one handfull and a half; seed of cardomums bruised 3 ounces; bay berries an ounce; put the seed into the vessel when it has wrought a while with the herbs, and after they are added, let the liquor work over the hogshead as little as may be; fill it at last, and before it is stopped put into the hogshead ten new-laid eggs, the shells not broken nor cracked; then stop it close and drink of it at two years' end, if it be carried by water it will be the better. But Doctor *Egidius* added water-cress, wild parsley, and six handfulls of horse-radish to each hogshead; and it was observed, the Mum which had in it the horse-radish drank more brisk than that which had not.

English Wines (1691).

BRUNSWICK MUM

Take sixty-three gallons of clear water that has been previously boiled to the reduction of a third part; then brew it with seven bushels of wheaten malt, and one bushel each of oatmeal and ground beans. When tunned, the hogshead must not be too full, and on its beginning to work, put in three pounds of fir and birch tops, three handfuls of the carduus benedictus, a handful or two or rose leaves, a handful and a half each of burnet, betony, savins, marjoram, pennyroyal, and mother of thyme, two or more handfuls of elder flowers, three ounces of bruised cardamoms, and an ounce of bruised barberries. The herbs and seeds are not to be put into the cask till the liquor has worked for some time, after which it should be suffered to flow over as little as possible. Lastly, fill it up on its ceasing to ferment, and when done, put in ten new-laid eggs unbroken or cracked, stop it up close, and at the end of two years it will be fit for use. To make mum like ale barley malt is substituted for wheat.

The New London Cookery (c. 1827).

NEGUS

One bottle of wine, half a pound of sugar or capillaire, and a sliced lemon or two fresh limes; add three quarts of boiling water, and grate nutmeg to taste.

ANOTHER WAY

Pour two quarts of boiling water upon three ounces of pearl barley, a quarter of a pound of sugar, and a lemon sliced; when cold, strain the liquor, and add a pint of wine and a glass of brandy.

Indian Domestic Economy (1849).

ENGLISH NOYEAU

Blanch and bruise a quarter of a pound of bitter almonds, or peach, or apricot kernels, put them into a pint of cold water, and let them stand two hours; then add three pints of white currant juice, three pounds of loaf sugar, the peels of three lemons grated, and a gallon of brandy. Stir them well together, let them stand three days, then strain off the liquor through a jelly-bag, and bottle it for use. A quart of fresh brandy put on the dregs and strained off, after standing three days longer, will make a very pleasant liquor for giving a flavour to puddings.

Anthony Haselmore (1823).

NOYEAU

Two gallons of gin, two pounds of bitter almonds, one pound of sweet almonds; pound them in a mortar, and beat to a fine paste; six pounds of powdered sugar (mix some with the almonds), let these stand ten days in the gin; filter through blotting-paper, and bottle it.

Bishop (1860).

HOME-MADE NOYEAU

Ingredients: 2 oz. of bitter almonds, 1 oz. of sweet ditto, 1 lb. of loaf sugar, the rinds of 3 lemons, 1 quart of Irish whiskey or gin, 1 tablespoonful of clarified honey, ½ pint of new milk.

Mode: Blanch and pound the almonds, and mix with them the sugar, which should also be pounded. Boil the milk; let it stand till quite cold; then mix all the ingredients together, and let them remain for 10 days, shaking them every day. Filter the mixture through blotting-paper, bottle off for use in small bottles, and seal the corks down. This will be found useful for flavouring many sweet dishes.

Average cost: 2s. 9d.

Sufficient to make about 2½ pints of noyeau.

Seasonable: May be made at any time.

Mrs. Beeton (1861).

ORANGE

The citrus fruit which shares with the lemon the greatest share of popularity in the British Isles. There are different varieties of oranges, of which the *Citrus aurentium*, or sweet orange, is the favourite as dessert fruit, *Citrus bigaradia*, or

Seville orange for marmalade and preserves, and *Citrus bergamia*, or bergamot orange for cordials and liqueurs.

TO MAKE CORDIAL ORANGE-WATER

Take one dozen and a half of the highest coloured and thick rind oranges, slice them thin, and put them into two pints of Malaga sack, and one pint of the best brandy, of cinnamon, nutmegs, ginger, cloves and mace, of each one quarter of an ounce bruised, of spearmint and balm, one handful of each, put them into an ordinary still all night, pasted up with rye paste; the next day draw them with a slow fire and keep a wet cloth upon the neck of the still; put in some loaf sugar into the glass where it drops.

Queen-like Closet, Hannah Wolley (1672).

TO MAKE ORANGE WINE

Put twelve pounds of fine sugar, and the whites of eight eggs well beaten, into six gallons of spring water, let it boil an hour, scumming it all the time, then take it off, and when it is pretty cool, put it to the juice of fifty Seville oranges, and six spoonfuls of good ale yeast and let it stand two days; then put it into another vessel, with two quarts of Rhenish wine, and the juice of twelve lemons; you must let the juice of the lemons and the wine, and two pounds of double refined sugar, stand close covered ten or twelve hours before you put into your vessel to your orange wine, and scum off the seeds before you put it in. The lemon peels must be put in with the oranges, half the rinds must be put into the vessel. It must stand ten or twelve days before it is fit to bottle.

The British Jewel (1782).

ORANGE WINE

Take 10 gallons of spring water and boil in it 30 lb. of loaf sugar and the whites of 6 or 8 eggs well beaten and put to it cold, taking off the scum as it rises, take it off the fire and put it in a clean tub. When almost cold put to it the juice of 100 Seville oranges with 2 or 3 white bread toasts spread with ale yeast. Let it stand 24 hours to ferment then add half the peel of your oranges, put the peel with the liquor into the vessel, cover the bung-hole with a piece of brown paper, and when fine rack it which is in about 3 or 4 months. When you put it

in the vessel again add to it a quart of French brandy. In
12 months it will be fit to drink out of the vessel or to bottle.
N.B.—To a quartern vessel put 2 quarts of brandy.

*MS. Book of Recipes, A*1 (1833).

EXCELLENT ORANGE WINE

Take half a chest of Seville oranges, pare off the rinds as
thin as possible, put two-thirds of them into six gallons of water,
and let them remain for twenty-four hours. Squeeze the
oranges (which ought to yield seven or eight quarts of juice)
through a sieve into a pan, and as they are done throw them
into six gallons more of water; let them be washed well in it
with the hands, and then put into another six gallons of water
and left till the following day. For each gallon of wine, put
into the cask three pounds and a quarter of loaf sugar, and the
liquor strained clear from the rinds and pulp. Wash these
again and again, should more liquor be required to fill the cask;
but do not at any time add raw water. Stir the wine daily
until the sugar is perfectly dissolved, and let it ferment from
four to five weeks; add to it two bottles of brandy, stop it down,
and in twelve months it will be fit to bottle.

Obs. The excellence of all wine depends so much upon the
fermentation being properly conducted, that unless the mode of
regulating this be understood by the maker, there will always
be great danger of failure in the operation. There is, we believe,
an excellent work upon the subject by Mr. McCulloch, which
the reader who needs information upon it will do well to con-
sult : our own experience is too slight to enable us to multiply
our receipts.

Eliza Acton (1854).

ORANGE-FLOWER RATAFIA (A DELICIOUS LIQUEUR)

Boil to a thick syrup a pound and a quarter of highly refined
sugar, and three-quarters of a pint of water; throw into it three
ounces of the petals only, plucked one by one from the stems,
of some freshly gathered orange-blossoms, give them two
minutes boil, take them from the fire, and when the whole is
half cold stir in two bottles of white French brandy; turn the
mixture into a new and well-scalded stone pitcher, or jar, make
it airtight as soon as the liqueur is quite cold, and in from three

to four weeks it will be ready to bottle after the flowers have been strained from it : they give it a delicious flavour.

Water, ¾ pint; sugar 1¼ lb.; 15 to 20 minutes, or more. Petals of the orange-blossom, 3 oz.; 2 minutes. White French brandy, 2 quarts : infuse 3 to 4 weeks.

Mrs. Acton (1854).

PARFAIT AMOUR

Pound the rinds of three cederaties (or citrons), or of four lemons in a mortar; and infuse them, with a quarter of an ounce of cochineal, in three quarts of brandy, for twenty-four hours. Melt two pounds of sugar in six quarts of boiling water; and, when dissolved, throw into the syrup eighteen pounded bitter almonds. Pour the syrup into the brandy; add a dram and a half of cinnamon, and three teaspoonfuls of coriander seeds. The following day dissolve a quarter of a dram each of roche allum, and crystal mineral, in a glass of hot water, and pour off the clear of it into the composition; let the liquor stand six days, and then run it through a flannel jelly-bag.

Duncan Macdonald, New London Family Cook (c. 1800).

PERFETTO AMORE, OR PERFECT LOVE

Infuse for twelve hours the yellow rind finely shred, of four Seville oranges, or half a dozen lemons, in a gallon of the best French brandy, with a handful of currants, a dozen coriander seeds, as many cloves, some cinnamon, and a very little salt. Draw off only two bottles of spirits; then take two pounds of sugar, boiled and clarified, in two bottles of water with three eggs; take a little roche allum, which you must mix in a little boiling water and some cream of tartar; mix them in a small mortar; then put it in the liqueur, but first strain it; then mix all together, and filter through blotting-paper.

Duncan Macdonald, New London Cook (c. 1800).

PARSNIP

This very old favourite among winter root vegetables is not nearly so popular to-day as it used to be, nor is it cultivated to the same extent as formerly, when the roots were used to make a "wine superior to all other home-made wines," as well as a kind of beer, with hops.

PARSNIP WINE

To every four pounds of parsnips, cleaned and quartered, put a gallon of water. Boil till they are quite soft, and strain the liquor clear off without crushing the parsnips. To every gallon of the liquor put three pounds of loaf-sugar, and a half ounce of crude tartar. When nearly cold, put fresh yeast to it. Let it stand four days in a warm room, and then bung it up.

N.B.—Parsnip-wine is said to surpass all the other home-made wines as much as East-India Madeira does that of the Cape. So much is said for it, and on good authority, that it certainly deserves a trial. Horseradish-wine is made as above, and is recommended for gouty habits. In Ireland a pleasant table-beer is made from parsnips brewed with hops.

Cook and Housewife's Manual (1829).

PEACH

This is perhaps the most delicious stone fruit grown in the British Isles, mostly under glass, although there are many places where peaches will ripen in the open in all except the more disappointing summers. One would be inclined to believe that the English climate must have deteriorated since the latter part of the seventeenth century, when peaches and apricots apparently grew so freely that there were enough and to spare for making into some sort of a wine.

WINE OF PEACH AND APRICOTS

Take of peaches, nectarines, etc., when they are full of juice, pare them, and quit them of their stones, then slice them thin, and put about a gallon to two gallons of water, and a quart of white wine, put them over a fire gently to simmer a considerable time, till the sliced fruit become soft, then pour off the liquid part into other peaches that have been so used and bruised, but not heated, let them stand twelve hours, sometimes with stirring, and then pour out the liquid part, and press what remains through a fine hair bag, and put them together into a cask to ferment, then add of loaf sugar a pound and a half to each gallon; boil well an ounce of beaten cloves in a quart of white wine, and add it to give a curious flavour.

Wine of apricots may be made with only bruising, and pouring the hot liquor upon, not requiring so much sweetening by reason they are of a more dulcid, or luscious quality, only to give it a curious flavour, boil an ounce of mace, and half an ounce of nutmegs in a quart of white wine, and when the wine is on the ferment, pour the liquid part in hot, and hang a bunch of fresh borage well flowered into the cask by a string at the bung for three days, then draw it off, and keep it in bottles, which are most proper to preserve these sorts of wines.

Their virtues. They are moderately warming and restorative, very good in consumptions, to create an appetite, and recover decayed and wasting bodies; they loosen the hardness of the belly, and give ease to the pains of the stomach.

The Way to get Wealth (1706).

PENNYROYAL

The name by which one of the mints (*Mentha pulegium*) used to be very popular in England, being regarded as an excellent cure for coughs and colds.

PENNYROYAL WATER

Gather your pennyroyal full grown, but before it is in blossom. Fill your cold still with it, and put it half full of water. Make a moderate fire under it, and distil it off cold. Then put it into bottles, and after two or three days, cork it up for use.

Anthony Haselmore (1823).

PERSICO

To four bottles of brandy, put four handfuls of the best fresh bitter almonds; cut them in small bits, add a little salt, two cloves, and some cinnamon; put all in the brandy, and infuse them for twenty hours; take two bottles of spirits; two pounds of sugar, with two bottles of water, without clarifying it, as this liquor will clarify itself.

Duncan Macdonald, New London Family Cook (c. 1800).

POPPY

One of the most decorative flowering weeds, the seeds of which have been used to make a kind of cordial.

POPPY BRANDY

Take six quarts of the best and freshest poppies, cut off the black ends of them and put them into a glass jar which will hold two gallons, and press them in it; then pour upon it a gallon of brandy, stop the glass close, and set it in the sun for a week or more. Afterwards squeeze out the poppies with your hands, and sweeten it to your taste with loaf sugar. Put to it an ounce of alkermes, perfumed, mix it well together, and bottle it.

J. Davies (1811).

CORDIAL POPPY WATER

Put a peck of poppies and two gallons of good brandy into a wide-mouthed glass; let them stand forty-eight hours, and then strain them. Stone a pound of sun raisins, and take an ounce of coriander seed, an ounce of sweet fennel seeds, and an ounce of liquorice sliced; bruise all together, put them into the brandy, with a pound of good powdered sugar, and let them stand four or eight weeks, shaking them every day; then strain it off, and bottle it close for use.

Duncan Macdonald, New London Family Cook (c. 1800).

ALE-POSSET

Boil a pint of new milk with a slice of toasted bread, sweeten and season a bottle of mild ale in a china basin or dish, and pour the boiling milk over it. When the head rises serve it.

Cook and Housewife's Manual (1829).

SACK POSSET

Take four ounces of pounded sugar, a pint of sherry and some grated nutmeg; warm them over the fire until the sugar is dissolved; then beat up ten fresh eggs, and strain them into a quart of new milk that has been boiled (but stood until cool), and add the wine and sugar; put the whole in to a clean saucepan on the fire, and keep stirring until it is nearly boiled, when remove, or it will curdle.

Indian Domestic Economy (1849).

PRINCE'S CORDIAL

For three gallons, take two quarts of cherry brandy, one quart of raspberry brandy, one quart of raisin wine, one gallon of spirits, six pennyweights of the acid of vitriol, ten drops of the oil of caraway, ten drops of the essence of lemon, half a pint of the spirit of wine, and one pound and a half of sugar. Fill up with water. Fine it with alum and salt of tartar.

For three gallons, take one quart of cherry brandy, one gallon of malt spirit, one quart of red-currant wine, one quart of orange wine, half an ounce of mace, a quarter of an ounce of orange wine, half an ounce of mace, a quarter of an ounce of cloves, a quarter of an ounce of cinnamon, half an ounce of coriander seeds, half an ounce of caraway seeds, four drops of the oil of orange, four drops of the essence of lemon, and two pounds of loaf sugar. Fill up with water.

N.B.—The mace, cloves, cinnamon, caraway and coriander seeds must be bruised in a mortar, and steeped in the spirit for five or six days. The oil and essence must be killed the same way as for gin. Colour with burnt sugar.

J. Davies (1811).

QUEEN'S CORDIAL

For three gallons, take seven quarts of malt spirit, one pennyweight and a half of the oil of mint, one pennyweight of the oil of caraway; one ounce of coriander seeds, one ounce of caraway seeds, half an ounce of cassia, a quarter of an ounce of mace, one pint of spirit of wine, and two pounds of loaf sugar. Fill up with water.

N.B.—The seeds, cassia, and mace must be bruised, and steeped in the spirit for three or four days, and well shaked twice a day. The oils must be killed as for gin. Fine with alum only.

J. Davies (1811).

QUINCE

The quince, the "Golden Apple" of the Ancients, who looked upon it as the emblem of love and happiness, is a fruit from the Mediterranean and Caucasus regions. Its cultivation spread to the West at an early date, and Chaucer speaks of it as being grown in England in his day. Quince is either round or pear-shaped, with yellow skin; the flesh is also yellow, but it turns pink in the cooking.

WINE OF QUINCES

Gather the quinces when pretty ripe, in a dry day, rub off the down with a clean linen cloth, then lay them in hay or straw for ten days to sweat, so cut them in quarters, and take out the core and bruise them well in a mashing tub with a wooden beetle and squeeze out the liquid part, by pressing them in a hair bag by degrees in a cider-press, strain this liquor through a fine sieve, then warm it gently over a fire, and scum it, but suffer it not to boil, sprinkle into it loaf-sugar reduced to powder, then in a gallon of water, and a quart of white wine, boil a dozen or fourteen large quinces thinly sliced, add two pounds of fine sugar, and then strain out the liquid part, and mingle it with the natural juice of the quinces put it into a cask not to fill it, and jumble them well together, then let it stand to settle, put in juice of Clary half a pint, to five or six gallons and mix it with a little flour and whites of eggs, so draw it off, and if it be not sweet enough, add more sugar, and a quart of the best Malmsey : you may, to make it better, boil a quarter of a pound of stoned raisins of the sun, and a quarter of an ounce of cinnamon in a quart of the liquor to the consumption of a third part, and straining the liquor, put it into the cask when the wine is upon the ferment.

Its Virtues. This wine is a good pectoral, cooling and re-freshing the vital parts; it is good, moderately taken in all hot diseases, allays the flushing of the face, and *S. Anthony's fire*, takes away inflammations, and is much available in breakings-out, botches, boils or sores.

The Way to get Wealth (1706).

TO MAKE QUINCE WINE

Gather your quinces when they are dry, take twenty large quinces, wipe them very clean with a coarse cloth, then grate them with a coarse grater or rasp, as near the core as you can, but grate in none of the core, nor the hard part of it, then boil a gallon of spring water, and put your grated quinces to it, and let it boil softly about a quarter of an hour, then strain the liquor into an earthen pot, and to each gallon of liquor put two pounds of fine loaf sugar, and stir it till your sugar is dis-solved; then cover it close, and let it stand twenty-four hours by which time it will be ready to bottle; take care that none of the settlement go into the bottles. This will keep good a year. Observe that your quinces must be very ripe when you gather them for this use.

The British Jewel (1782).

QUINCE WINE

Take your quinces when thoroughly ripe, wipe off the fur very clean, take out the cores, bruise and press them, add to every gallon of juice two pounds and a half of fine sugar; stir it together till it is dissolved, put it in your cask, and when it has done working, stop it close; let it stand six months before it is bottled. Keep it two or three years, and it will improve.

Anthony Haselmore (1823).

RAISINS

Raisins are grapes which have been sun-dried or dried by artificial means for storage and use at a later date. Not all grapes are suitable for drying into raisins, and until the latter part of the last century practically all raisins obtainable in England came from either Malaga or Greece. They are now sent to this country from Australia, South Africa, California, and other parts of the world, as well as Spain and Greece.

TO MAKE RAISIN WINE

Take two gallons of spring water and let it boil half an hour; then put into a stein pot two pounds of raisins stoned, two pounds of sugar, the rind of two lemons, and the juice of four; then pour the boiling water on the things in the stein, and let it stand covered four or five days; strain it out and bottle it up; in fifteen or sixteen days it will be fit to drink; it is a very cool pleasant drink in hot weather.

Gelleroy—London Cook (1762).

TO MAKE RAISIN WINE

To every gallon of clear Thames or other river water, put five pounds of Malaga or Belvedere raisins, let them steep a fortnight, stirring them every day, then pour the liquor off, and squeeze the juice of the raisins, and put both liquors together in a vessel that is of a size to contain it exactly, for it should be quite full; let the vessel stand open thus till the wine has done hissing, or making the least noise; you may add a pint of French brandy to every two gallons; then stop it close, and when you find it is fine, which you may know by pegging it, bottle it off.

If you would have it red, put one gallon of Alicant wine to every four of raisin wine.

The British Jewel (1782).

TO MAKE SMYRNA RAISIN WINE

To one hundred of raisins put twenty gallons of water, let it stand fourteen days, then put it into your cask; when it has been in six months, add to it one gallon of French brandy, and when it is fine then bottle it.

The Experienced English Housekeeper (1806).

RAISIN WINE WITH CIDER

Put two hundred weight of Malaga raisins into a cask, and pour upon them a hogshead of good sound cider that is not rough; stir it well two or three days; stop it, and let it stand six months; then rack into a cask that it will fill, and put in a gallon of the best brandy.

If raisin wine be much used, it would answer well to keep a cask always for it, and bottle off one year's wine just in time to make the next, which, allowing the six months of infusion, would make the wine to be eighteen months old. In cider counties this way is very economical; and even if not thought strong enough, the addition of another quarter of a hundred of raisins would be sufficient, and the wine would still be very cheap.

When the raisins are pressed through a horse-hair bag, they will either produce a good spirit by distillation, and must be sent to a chemist who will do it (but if for that purpose they must be very little pressed); or they will make excellent vinegar.

The stalks should be picked out for the above, and may be thrown into any cask of vinegar that is making; being very acid.

Domestic Cookery (1814).

RASPBERRIES

Cultivated raspberries are either red or yellow, but the red are the more extensively grown in England. Some varieties ripen their fruit in June and July, and others as late as October and even November, which means that they are available for a longer period each year than all other berries, with the exception of the alpine or "wild" strawberries.

WINE OF RASPBERRIES, THE ENGLISH WAY

Take what quantity you please of red raspberries when they are meanly ripe, for if they grow over-ripe, they will lose much

90

of their pleasant scent, and clearing the husks and stalks from them, soak them in the like quantity of fair water that has been boiled and sweetened with fine loaf sugar, a pound and a half to a gallon; when they are well soaked about twelve hours, take them out, put them up into a fine linen pressing bag, press out the juice into the water, then boil them up together, and scum them well twice or thrice over a gentle fire, take off the vessel, and let the liquor cool, and when the scum arises, take off all that you can, and pour off the liquor by inclination into a well-seasoned cask, or earthen vessel, then boil an ounce of mace very well in a pint of white-wine till the third part of the wine be consumed, strain it, and add it to the liquor; let it settle two days, and when it has well settled and fermented, draw it off into casks or bottles, and keep it in cool places.

The Way to get Wealth (1706).

RASPBERRY WINE, THE FRENCH WAY

Steep two gallons of raspberries in a gallon of sack, twenty-four hours, then strain them, and put to the liquor three-quarters of a pound of raisins of the sun well stoned, and so let them continue four or five days, sometimes stirring them well, then pour it off by inclination, that the clearest may be taken away, and only the dross and settlings remain in the bottom, and bottle that up you pour off, and if you find it not sweet enough for your palate, you may add some sugar, about half a pound to a gallon will be sufficient; keep these in a cool place.

Their virtues. These wines either way are a great cordial, they cleanse the blood, prevent pestilential air, comfort the heart, ease pains in the stomach, dispel gross vapours from the brain, cause free breathing by removing obstructions from the lungs, and successfully taken in apoplexy.

The Way to get Wealth (1706).

RASPBERRY WINE

Take ripe raspberries, crush them with your hands, and upon every gallon of the fruit pour one gallon (or if you would have the wine stronger, three quarts) of boiling water; let them infuse a day and night (stirring the liquor about twice a day), then strain it through a hair sieve, and to every gallon of this infusion, put two pound and a half of good sugar. Let it stand to dissolve twenty-four hours; stir the whole together, and if the fermentation do not proceed to your mind, barm it with a little yeast spread over a toast. Let the vessel be slightly covered over, until it has done working; then clay up the vessel close, and let it stand half a year (or longer, if it be not then fine enough), and at last bottle it.

Some persons in making this and other wines abounding with luxuriant juices, consisting of very active and fermenting particles, do use to draw it off from the lees before they put it into the cask they design to keep it in; and as often as that accident happens (*viz.* of fretting or fermenting anew) they repeat the operation of racking the liquor off; but how detrimental this proceeding is to the wine, both reason and experience will shew. For these dreggy parts are the most subtle and active principles of the liquor, whereon the wine (after the vessel is bunged down or close stopped up) begins to feed, and thereby daily improves in strength and goodness. But when by this method it is robbed of the same, we generally find that such liquors will not keep long before they turn flat and vapid. Therefore if these wines should by any accident happen to ferment anew, the only and most ready way to check it, is by burning sulphur under the cask, which immediately restrains and represses the fury of the fermentation, and causes the fermenting particles to subside. And upon this consideration it is, that others use to season their wine vessels with putting a lighted match of brimstone into them and afterwards rinsing them out with a little of the same (or any other wine) which is a good precaution against the recited accident, though not always to be depended upon.

It is remarked by some curious observers, that this berry affords a much thinner and more piercing wine than the brambleberry doth; whence it happens that they who drink this wine in any considerable quantity in the evening, generally perceive two notable effects from it the next morning, a reddish-coloured sweat, and violent pain in the head; which arise from the volatile salt and sulphur wherewith the raspberry abounds above most other fruits; and this made the learned *Hoffman* affirm, that this wine will greatly affect the head and occasion drunkenness; a necessary caution to be observed by those who are admirers of these liquors.

The Practical Distiller (1743).

A RECEIPT FOR RASPBERRY WINE

To every quart of fruit, you must pour, boiling hot, a quart of water, cover it very close, and let it stand twenty-four hours, then strain it, and to three quarts of the liquor, put two pounds of loaf sugar : stir it together and spread a toast of bread, the round of a loaf, with yeast, put it into it, which will set it to work, and in twenty-four hours pour it off the lees, and when it has quite done working stop it up; let it stand for six or seven months, you may bottle it, and keep it a year in bottles.

You must, at first, watch all wines, and if you find them fret, continue to fine them off the lees every day, for some time, as fast as any settles.

Daily Companion (1799).

RASPBERRY WINE

Take three pounds of raisins, wash, clean and stone them thoroughly; boil two gallons of spring water for half an hour; as soon as it is taken off the fire pour it into a deep stone jar, and put in the raisins, with six quarts of raspberries and two pounds of loaf sugar; stir it well together, and cover down closely, and set it in a cool place; stir it twice a day; then pass it through a sieve; put the liquor into a close vessel, adding one pound more loaf sugar; let it stand for a day and a night to settle, after which, bottle it, adding a little more sugar.

Bishop (1860).

TO MAKE RASPBERRY BRANDY

Gather the raspberries when the sun is hot upon them, and as soon as ever you have got them, to every five quarts of raspberries, put one quart of the best brandy, boil a quart of water five minutes with a pound of double refined sugar in it and pour it boiling hot on the berries, let it stand all night, then add nine quarts more brandy, stir it about very well, put it in a stone bottle, and let it stand a month or six weeks; when fine bottle it.

English Housekeeper (1806).

RASPBERRY BRANDY

Pick fine dry fruit, put into a stone jar, and the jar into a kettle of water, or on a hot hearth, till the juice will run; strain, and to every pint add half a pound of sugar, give one boil, and skim it; when cold, put equal quantities of juice and brandy, shake well, and bottle. Some people prefer it stronger of the brandy.

Domestic Cookery (1814).

RATAFIA

A generic name for a number of cordials, usually home-made, always sweet and often of very highly alcoholic strength. Ratafia may be made with new wine or grape juice and sufficient spirit to stop its fermentation; being further flavoured with various fruits, herbs and spices; or else by the infusion of the same ingredients in brandy.

"Every liqueur made by infusion is called Ratafia; that is when the spirit is made to imbibe thoroughly the aromatic flavour and colour of the fruit steeped in it; when this has taken place the liqueur is drawn off and sugar added to it; it is then filtered and bottled."

In early Victorian days the more popular ratafias were the orange, raspberry, currants, mulberries, green walnut.

RATAFIA

Get three gallons of molasses brandy, nuts two ounces and a half, bitter almonds one pound and a half, bruise them, and infuse them in a pint of brandy, adding three grains of amber-grease, mixed with three pounds of fine Lisbon sugar. Infuse all for seven days, and then strain it off for use.

The British Jewel (1782).

RATAFIA

For three gallons, take six quarts of rectified malt spirit, six grains of ambergris, two ounces of peach and apricot kernels, five ounces of bitter almonds, one pint and a half of spirit of wine, and two pounds of sugar. Fill up with water.

RATAFIA ANOTHER WAY

Take one quart of brandy, or good malt spirit, four ounces of apricot or peach kernels, a quarter of an ounce of bitter almonds; bruise your kernels in a mortar with a spoonful of brandy, and then put them together into a bottle with a quarter of a pound of loaf sugar; let it stand till it has imbibed the taste of the kernels, then pour it out into a bottle, and cork it close.

You may increase the quantity of spirit to your kernels, if you choose.

J. Davies (1811).

RED RATAFIA

Six pounds of the black-heart cherry, one of small black cherries or geens, and two of raspberries and strawberries. Bruise the fruit, and when it has stood some time, drain off the juice, and to every pint add four ounces of the best refined sugar, or of syrup, and a quart of the best brandy. Strain through a jelly-bag, and flavour to taste with a half-ounce of cinnamon and a drachm of cloves, bruised and infused in brandy for a fortnight before, or with cloves alone.

Cook and Housewife's Manual (1829).

COMMON RATAFIA

Take an ounce of bruised nutmegs, a half pound of bitter almonds, blanched and chopped, and a grain of ambergris, well rubbed with sugar in a mortar; infuse in two quarts of proof-spirit for two weeks, and filter.

Cook and Housewife's Manual (1829).

RATAFIA, OF FOUR FRUITS

Ten pounds of very ripe cherries, two pounds and a half of raspberries, five pounds and a half of red and two pounds and a half of black currants; pick and mix these fruits together, press the juice from them, measure it, and for every quart of juice take half a pound of sugar and an equal quantity of brandy; dissolve the sugar in the juice, then put in the brandy, and a drachm of mace and two drachms of cloves. Let the whole stand some time, filter, and bottle it. Keep them well corked.

Bishop (1860).

REGENTS

Pare, as thin as possible, the rinds of two China oranges, of two lemons and of one Seville orange, and infuse them for an hour in half a pint of thin cold syrup; then add to them the juice of the fruit; make a pint of strong green tea; sweeten it well with fine sugar, and when it is quite cold, add it to the fruit and syrup, with a glass of best old Jamaica rum, a glass of brandy, one of arrack, one of fine apple syrup and two bottles of the champagne; pass the whole through a fine lawn sieve until it is perfectly clear; then bottle and put it into ice until dinner is served.

Indian Domestic Economy (1849).

ROSE

The rose has been admired and loved by more people and during more centuries than any other flower. The Romans used to serve wine with rose petals floating on it, for the sake of their sweet scent, and when distillation was introduced in England, many tried to extract by this means their scent.

WINE OF ROSES

To do this, fit a glass basin or body, or for want of it a well-glazed earthen vessel, and put into it three gallons of rosewater drawn with a cold still, put into it a convenient quantity of roseleaves, cover it close, and put it for an hour in a kettle or cauldron of water, heating over the fire to take out the whole strength and tincture of the roses, and when cold press the roseleaves hard into the liquor, and steep fresh ones in, repeating it till the liquor has got a full strength of the roses, and then to every gallon of liquor, add three pounds of loaf-sugar, stir it well that it may melt and disperse in every part, then put it up into a cask, or other convenient vessel to ferment; and to make it do so the better, add a little fixed nitre and flour, and two or three whites of eggs, and let stand cool about thirty days, and it will be ripe and have a curious flavour, having the whole strength and scent of the roses in it and you may add to ameliorate in some wine and spices, as your taste or inclination leads you.

And this by way of infusion : wine of carnations, cloves, gillyflowers, violets, primroses, or any flower having a curious scent may be made, to which, to prevent repetition, and go on with as much brevity as conveniently may be, I refer you.

The Virtues. Wines thus made, are not only pleasant in taste, but rich and medicinal, being excellent for strengthening the heart, refreshing the spirits, and gently cooling the body, making it lenitive and so purges the first digestion of phlegm, sometimes choler, abates the heat of the fever, quenches thirst, mitigates the inflammation of the entrails, and may, on sundry occasions, serve for a good counter-poison.

The Way to get Wealth (1706).

ROSE WINE

Put into a well-glazed earthen vessel three quarts of rose-water, drawn with a cold still, put into it a sufficient quantity of roseleaves, cover it close, and set it for an hour in a kettle, or copper of hot water, to take out the whole strength and flavour of the roses. When it is cold, press roseleaves hard into the liquor, and steep fresh ones in it, repeating it till the liquor has got the full strength of the roses; to every gallon of liquor put three pounds of loaf-sugar, and stir it well, that it may melt and disperse in every part; then put it into a cask or other convenient vessel to ferment, and throw into it a piece of bread toasted hard and covered with yeast; let it stand a month, when it will be ripe and have all the fine flavour and scent of the roses; if you add some wine and spices it will be a considerable improvement.

By the same mode of infusion wine may be made from any other flowers that have an odoriferous scent, and grateful flavour. In all made wines, brandy will be found more useful than Rhenish wine, as the latter is apt to turn it sour.

A brandy cask is also useful.

Daily Companion (1799).

ROSE WATER

The roses should be gathered when dry and full-blown, pick off the leaves, and to every peck put a quart of water. Then put them into a cold still, and make a slow fire under it for the slower it is distilled the better it will be. Bottle it, and in two or three days cork it for use.

The New London Cookery (c. 1827).

ROSEMARY

Rosemary is one of the most universally cultivated of garden herbs; it is to be found in practically every cottage garden, which hardly bears out the old saying that rosemary refuses to grow except in the gardens of the virtuous. It possesses a very pungent, rather gingery, smell, and is best used in strict moderation; otherwise its scent may be somewhat aggressive, although never offensive.

TO MAKE ROSEMARY WATER

Take a quart of sack or white wine with as many rosemary flowers as will make it very thick, two nutmegs, and two races

of ginger sliced thin into it; let it infuse all night, then distil
it in an ordinary still as your other waters.
Queen-like Closet, Hannah Wolley (1672).

RUMFUSTIAN
Rumfustian is prepared at Oxford as follows : whisk up to
a froth the yolks of six eggs and add them to a pint of gin and
a quart of strong beer; boil up a bottle of sherry in a saucepan
with a stick of cinnamon or nutmeg grated, a dozen large lumps
of sugar, and the rind of a lemon peeled very thin; when the
wine boils, it is poured upon the beer and gin and drank hot.
Indian Domestic Economy (1849).

SAGE
Sage may be said to have been the precursor of tea, in England.
When it was introduced, in the sixteenth century, it had an
immediate and widespread popularity; it was mostly drunk
hot, like tea, but it was also used to make wines and cordials :
it was also used to flavour butter, cheese, stuffings, sauces
and stews.

TO MAKE EXCELLENT SAGE WINE
Take six pound of sage picked, shred it very small, pour
upon it three gallons of boiling hot water, cover it close and let
it stand four and twenty hours, then press it out, and to every
gallon put a pound and a half of clear sugar, or a quart of the
syrup or sweets mentioned at the Sect. XIII, put it up into
a cask, and it will work, cover it loosely, or with a plate of lead
upon the bung, and let it stand six weeks, or till you see it has
quite done working, then bottle it. The best way to make
this sage wine is to stamp or pound the sage in a stone mortar,
and then pour your liquor boiling hot upon it, and cover close
for twelve or sixteen hours, then press it out, and thus you
have all the juice of the sage. Sage wine is good for women
with child to prevent abortion. In like manner you may make
clary wine and balm wine, either shredding or stamping the
herbs. You may make it also by boiling your water and sugar
together, and then pour it boiling hot upon your herbs.
If any think it too much trouble for themselves to prepare
the sweets or syrup before mentioned, they may have them at
almost every sugar-bakers in London.
The Family Physitian (1696).

HOW TO MAKE SAGE WINE
Boil twenty-six quarts of spring water a quarter of an hour, and when it is blood warm put twenty-five pounds of Malaga raisins, picked, rubbed and shred into it, with almost half a bushel of sage shred, and a porringer of ale yeast; stir all well together and let it stand in a tub, covered warm six or seven days, stirring it every day; then strain it off and put it in a runlet, let it work three or four days, and then stop it up. When it has stood six or seven days, put in a quart or two of Malaga sack, and when it is fine bottle it.

The British Jewel (1782).

SAGE WINE I
Boil six gallons of spring water a quarter of an hour, let it cool till it is milk-warm, and put in twenty-five pounds of Malaga raisins, picked and rubbed clean, and cut small, together with half a bushel of red sage cut small, and a gill of ale yeast : stir them all well together, and let them stand covered in a warm place six or seven days, stirring them once a day. After which strain the liquor into a clean cask, and when it has worked three or four days, bung it up, and let it stand about a week longer; then put into it two quarts of mountain wine, with a gill of finings, and when fine bottle it.

SAGE WINE II
Take thirty pounds of Malaga raisins, picked clean and cut small, and one bushel of green sage cut small : then boil six gallons of water, letting it stand till it is milk-warm : after which you must pour it into tub upon your sage and raisins, and let it stand five or six days, stirring it twice a day : then strain out the liquor from the pulp, put it into a cask, and let it stand six months. Afterwards draw it clear off into another cask, and when fine bottle it. In two months it will be fit for use, but will improve by being kept a year.

J. Davies (1811).

SCURVY GRASS
One of the common grasses which grows in most parts of the British Isles and is also known as spoonwort, the approximation of its botanical name *Cochlearia*. Its leaves are succulent

and acceptable in salads; the stems are juicy and rather bitter, but pleasantly so. Scurvy grass used to enjoy a high reputation as a remedy for many ills.

SCURVY-GRASS WINE

Scurvy-grass, or spoonwort, is a very sovereign medicinable herb, appropriated chiefly to the health of English bodies, in many medicines cheerful; the wine made of it containing all its virtues with addition, must needs be very acceptable. To make it then:

Take the best large scurvy-grass tops and leaves in May, June, or July, bruise them well in a stone mortar, then put it in a well-glazed earthen vessel, and sprinkle it over with some powder of crystal or tartar, then smear it over with virgin honey and being covered close let it stand twenty-four hours, then set water over a gentle fire, putting to every gallon three pints of honey, and when the scum rises, take it off, and let it cool, then put your stamped scurvy-grass into a barrel, and pour the liquor to it, setting the vessel conveniently endways, with a tap at the bottom, and when it has been infused twenty-four hours, draw off the liquor, and strongly press the juice and moisture out of the herb into the barrel or vessel, and so put the liquor up again; then put a little new ale yeast to it and suffer it to ferment three days, covering the place of the bung or vent, with a piece of bread spread over with mustard-seed downward in a cool place, and so let it continue till it is fine, and drinks brisk, then is your time to draw off the finest part, leaving only the dregs behind; add more herbs, and so ferment with white of eggs, flour, and fixed nitre, verjuice, or the juice of green grapes, if they be to be had, to which add six pounds of the syrup of mustard, all mixed and well beaten together to refine it down, and it will drink brisk, but is not very toothsome : being inserted among artificial wines rather for the health of persons than for the delightfulness of gust.

Its virtues. It helps digestion, warms cold stomachs, carries off phlegm, purifies the blood, purges out salt watery humours, cleanses the bowels from cold sliminess, eases pains in the limbs, head, heart and stomach; as also those pricking pains that are occasioned by scorbutic humours.

The Way to get Wealth (1706).

TO MAKE SHERBET

Take nine Seville oranges and three lemons, grate off the yellow rinds and put the raspings into a gallon of water, and three pounds of double refined sugar, and boil it to a candy height, then take it off the fire, and put in the juice and the pulp of the above, and keep stirring it until it is almost cold, then put it in a pot for use.

TO MAKE FINE SHERBET A SECOND WAY

Pare four large lemons, and boil the peels in six quarts of water and a little ginger cut fine, boil them a quarter of an hour then add to it three pounds of sugar, and when it is cold put in the juice of the lemons and strain it, and it is fit for use.

TO MAKE SHERBET A THIRD WAY

Take twelve quarts of water to six pounds of Malaga raisins, slice six lemons into it, with one pound of sixpenny sugar, put them all together into an earthen pan, let it stand three days, stirring it three times a day, then take them out, and let them drain in a flannel bag, and then bottle it; do not fill the bottles too full lest they burst. It will be fit to drink in about a fortnight.

English Housekeeper (1806).

TO MAKE SHRUB FOR PUNCH

Take the peels of five lemons, infuse them in a quart of brandy; then add the juice of ten lemons, with half a pound of loaf sugar; stir all well together, and let them stand for twenty-four hours, then strain the liquor through a jelly-bag, for use.

To a quart of this infusion, you may put one pint of brandy, and three quarts of spring water, and the punch is made. But it is to be observed, that all the lemons are to be perfectly sound; for one faulty lemon will spoil the whole composition.

The Practical Distiller (1734).

TO MAKE CURRANT SHRUB

Pick your currants clean from the stalks when they are full ripe, and put twenty-four pounds into a pitcher, with two pounds of single refined sugar, close the jug well up, and put it into a pan of boiling water till they are soft, then strain them through a jelly-bag, and to every quart of juice put one quart of brandy, a pint of red wine, one quart of new milk, a pound of double refined sugar, and the whites of two eggs well beat, mix them all together, and cover them close up two days, then run it through a jelly-bag and bottle it for use.

English Housekeeper (1806).

SHRUB BRANDY

Put two quarts of brandy into a large bottle, with the juice of five lemons and the peels of two; stop it up, and let it stand three days; then add three pints of white wine, a pound and a half of loaf-sugar and half a nutmeg; strain it through a flannel bag, and it will be found excellent.

Indian Domestic Economy (1849).

TO MAKE ALMOND SHRUB

Take three gallons of rum or brandy, three quarts of orange juice, the peels of three lemons, three pounds of loaf sugar, then take four ounces of bitter almonds, blanch and beat them fine, mix them in a pint of milk, then mix them all well together, let it stand an hour to curdle, run it through a flannel bag several times till it is clear, then bottle it for use.

English Housekeeper (1806).

STRAWBERRIES

The strawberry grows in one form or another in every part of the world, from the arctic regions to the tropics. There has been a wild kind of strawberry growing in the British Isles from the earliest times, and many sorts have also been cultivated during the past five hundred years. In the Star Chamber Accounts and other ancient documents, wild strawberries are called "strawberries" whilst the cultivated ones are always referred to as "garden strawberries."

STRAWBERRY WINE

Bruise the strawberries, and put them into a linen-bag which has been used a little, that the liquor may run through more easily. You hang in the bag at the bung into the vessel before you do put in your strawberries. The quantity of the fruit is left to your discretion; for you will judge to be there enough of them when the colour of the wine is high enough. During the working you leave the bung open. The working being over

you stop your vessel. Cherry-wine is made after the same fashion. But it is a little more troublesome to break the cherry-stones. But it is necessary that if your cherries be of the black sour cherries. You put to it a little cinnamon, and a few cloves.
Sir Kenelme Digby (1669).

SURFEIT WATER

Take Roman wormwood, scurvy-grass, brook-lime, water-cresses, balm, sage, mint, rue, and chives, of each one hand-ful; poppies, if fresh, half a peck; but if dry, half that quantity; cochineal and saffron, sixpennyworth of each; anniseeds, carra-way, coriander, and cardamum seeds, of each an ounce; two ounces of scraped liquorice, split figs, and raisins of the sun stoned, of each a pound, juniper berries bruised, beaten nutmeg, mace bruised and sweet fennel seeds also bruised, of each an ounce; a few flowers of rosemary, marigold, and sage. Put these into a large stone jar, and pour on them three gallons of French brandy. Cover it close, and let it stand near the fire for three weeks, stirring it three times a week. Then strain it off. Bottle your liquor, and pour on the ingredients a quart more of French brandy. Let it stand a week, stirring it once a day; then distil it in a cold still, and you will have a fine white surfeit water. Bottle it close, and it will retain its virtues a long time.
Anthony Haselmore (1823).

SYCAMORE WINE

To every gallon of the liquor fresh drawn from the tree, and boiled a quarter of an hour over the fire, add two pounds of the finest powdered sugar. Boil the liquor again for half an hour longer, taking off all the scum as it rises. When re-moved from the fire, and almost cold, barm it as you do birch-wine; let it stand until it be white over, stirring it twice a day (*viz.* for three or four days), then smoke your barrel with a little brimstone : and when you tun it, put into each gallon of liquor one pound of Malaga raisins, clean picked and shredded (or a like quantity of loaf sugar), with the whites of two eggs. Stop it up close, and let it remain unmoved until the wine be perfectly fine, and then bottle it.

Note: That this sycamore wine, after it has stood a due time upon the raisins, is to be racked off into a clean cask, and

depurated with isinglass, as directed in the making of birch-wine, if it be not then clear. You may gather the water or juice of the sycamore tree, for making this wine, in January.
The Practical Distiller (1734).

TO MAKE SYCAMORE WINE

Take two gallons of the sap and boil it half an hour, then add to it four pounds of fine powder sugar, beat the whites of three eggs to a froth, and mix them with the liquor, but if it be too hot, it will poach the eggs, scum it very well, and boil it half an hour, then strain it through a hair sieve, and let it stand till next day, then pour it clean from the sediments, put half a pint of good yeast to every twelve gallons, cover it up close with blankets till it is white over, then put it into the barrel, and leave the bung-hole open till it has done working, then close it well up, let it stand three months, then bottle it, the fifth part of the sugar must be loaf, and if you like raisins, they are a great addition to the wine.

N.B.—You may make birch wine the same way.
English Housekeeper (1806).

TO MAKE VIN DE MOLOSSO, OR TREACLE WINE

Take fair water and make it so strong with molasses, otherwise called treacle, as that it will bear an egg, then boil it with a bag of all kinds of spices, and a branch or two of rosemary, boil it and scum it and put in some sweet herbs or flowers, according to the time of the year, boil it till a good part be consumed, and that it be very clear, then set it to cool in several things, and when it is almost cold, work it with yeast as you do beer, the next day put it into a vessel, and so soon as it has done working stop it up close; and when it has stood a fortnight, bottle it; this is a very wholesome drink against any infection, or for any that are troubled with the prisick.
Queen-like Closet, Hannah Wolley (1672).

TURNIP

Turnips belong to two main classes which are distinguished by the shape of the roots : the best, as regards the juiciness of the roots, are the long-rooted turnips; the others have flat or round roots.

TO MAKE TURNIP WINE

Take a good many turnips, pare them, slice them, and put them into a cider-press, and press out all the juice very well; to every gallon of juice have three pounds of lump sugar; have a vessel ready, just big enough to hold the juice, put your sugar into the vessel, and to every gallon of the juice put half a pint of brandy; pour in the juice, and lay something over the bung for a week, to see if it works; if it does you must not bung it down till it has done working, then stop it close for three months, and draw it off into another vessel. When it is fine bottle it off.

The British Jewel (1872).

USQUEBAUGH, THE IRISH CORDIAL

To two quarts of the best brandy, or whisky without a smoky taste, put a pound of stoned raisins, a half-ounce of nutmegs, a quarter-ounce of cloves, the same quantity of cardamoms, all bruised in a mortar; the rind of a Seville orange, rubbed off on lumps of sugar, a little tincture of saffron, and a half-pound of brown candy-sugar. Shake the infusion every day for a fortnight, and filter it for use.

Obs. Not a drop of water must be put to Irish cordial. It is sometimes tinged of a fine green with the juice of spinage, instead of the saffron tint, from which it takes the name (as we conjecture) of *usquebeœ*, or yellow water.

Cook and Housewife's Manual (1829).

VINES

BRISK WINE FROM THE LEAVES AND TENDRILS OF THE VINE

An excellent brisk wine may be made from the leaves and tendrils of the vine. The leaves are best when young, at farthest they should not have attained their full growth, and they should be plucked with their stems. To make ten gallons of wine, Dr. Macculloch directs to pour seven or eight gallons of boiling water upon forty or fifty pounds of the leaves into a tub of sufficient capacity, and to suffer the leaves to macerate for twenty-four hours. The liquor being poured off, the leaves must be submitted to a press of considerable power, and being subsequently washed with an additional gallon of water, they must again be pressed. The quantity of sugar to be employed may vary as in the former recipes from twenty-five to thirty pounds, and the quantity being made up to ten gallons and a half, the process recommended for making gooseberry wine is to be followed.

The New London Cookery (1827).

WALNUT WATER, OR THE WATER OF LIFE

Take green walnuts in the beginning of June, beat them in a mortar, and distil them in an ordinary still, keep that water by itself, then about Midsummer gather some more, and distil them as you did before, keep that also by itself, then take a quart of each and mix them together, and distil them in a glass still, and keep it for your use; the virtues are as follows : It will help all manner of dropsies and palsies, drank with wine fasting; it is good for the eyes, if you put one drop therein; it helps conception in women if they drink thereof one spoonful at a time in a glass of wine once a day, and it will make your skin fair if you wash therewith; it is good for all infirmities of the body, and drives out all corruption, and inward bruises; if it is drunk with wine moderately, it kills worms in the body, whoever drinks much of it, shall live so long as Nature shall continue in him.

Finally, if you have any wine that is turned, put in a little vial or glass full of it, and keep it close stopped, and within four days it will come to itself again.

Queen-like Closet, Hannah Wolley (1672).

WALNUT WINE

To every gallon of water, put four pounds of honey, and to twenty gallons, put one pound of walnut-leaves, dried. Boil it a full hour, and scum it well; then run the liquor through a sieve, and when it is cold and settled, tun it into the vessel; stop it up as soon as it has done hissing; let it stand in the cask a year, then bottle it.

N.B.—The leaves must be gathered in July, and used in September.

Addison Ashburn (1807).

WHISKEY CORDIAL

Ingredients: 1 lb. of ripe white currants, the rind of 2 lemons, ¼ oz. of grated ginger, 1 quart of whiskey, 1 lb. of lump sugar.

Mode: Strip the currants from the stalks; put them into a large jug; add the lemon-rind, ginger, and whiskey; cover the jug closely, and let it remain covered for 24 hours. Strain through a hair sieve, add the lump sugar, and let it stand 12 hours longer; then bottle, and cork well.

Time: To stand 24 hours before being strained; 12 hours after the sugar is added.

Seasonable: Make this in July.

Mrs. Beeton (1861).

WORMWOOD

An aromatic herb (*Artemisia Absinthium*) with small, much cut, pale green leaves and small, round, yellow flowers. It grows wild in many waste places of the British Isles and it is also cultivated for use as a tonic and a flavouring agent in home-made cordials and liqueurs.

TO MAKE WORMWOOD WATER

Take four ounces of aniseeds, four ounces of licorice scraped, bruise them well with two ounces of nutmegs, add to them one good handful of wormwood, one root of angelica, steep them in three gallons of sack lees and strong ale together twelve hours then distil them in an alembeck, and keep it for your use.

Queen-like Closet, Hannah Wolley (1672).

WORMWOOD

For three gallons, take two gallons of rectified malt spirit; two pennyweights of the oil of orange, two pennyweights of the oil of caraway, one pennyweight of the oil of wormwood, a quarter of an ounce of almond cake, half an ounce of coriander seed, half an ounce of virginian snake root, half a pound of sugar; and fill up with water. Steep the coriander seed, almond cake, and virginian snake root, in the spirit for three or four days, and kill the oil as before mentioned.

J. Davies (1811).

IMITATIONS OF IMPORTED WINES

CHAMPAGNE

TO MAKE ENGLISH CHAMPAGNE OR THE FINE CURRANT WINE

To three gallons of water nine pounds of Lisbon sugar,
boil the water and sugar half an hour, skim it clean, then have
one gallon of currants picked but not bruised. Pour the
liquor boiling hot over them and when cold work it with half
a pint of yeast two days, then pour it through a flannel or sieve.
Put it in a barrel fit for it with half an ounce of isinglass well
bruised. When it has done working stop it close for a month
then bottle it, put a very small lump of double refined sugar.
This is an excellent wine and has a beautiful colour.

Wm. Gilleroy—London Cook (1762).

TO MAKE GOOSEBERRY WINE LIKE CHAMPAGNE

To every gallon of water, put four pounds of gooseberries
(when fit to bottle); bruise them well, and let them stand in
the water three or four days, stirring them twice a day; then
strain it through a sieve, and to every gallon of liquor, put
three pounds of loaf sugar, and to every five gallons, a bottle
of the best brandy; put it immediately into the cask, and stop
it close; let it stand six months, then bottle it; let it stand in
the bottles six months, and it will be fit for use.

Addison Ashburn (1807).

BRITISH CHAMPAGNE

Take eight pounds of white sugar; the whitest raw sugar, seven
ditto; crystallized lemon acid or tartaric-acid, an ounce and

a quarter; pure water, eight gallons; white grape wine, two quarts, or perry, four quarts; of French brandy, three pints. Boil the sugars in the water, skimming it occasionally for two hours, then pour it into a tub, and dissolve in it the acid. Before it is cold, add some yeast, and ferment in the same manner as directed for Maderia. Put it in a cask, and add the other ingredients. Bung it well, and keep it in a cool place for two or three months; bottle it, and keep it cool for a month longer when it will be fit for use. If not perfectly clear after standing in the cask two or three months, render it so by use of isinglass before it is bottled.

By adding a pound of fresh or preserved strawberries, and two ounces of powdered cochineal, to the above quantity, the pink champagne may be made.

Anthony Haselmore (1823).

BEST WHITE GOOSEBERRY CHAMPAGNE

To every Scotch pint of ripe white gooseberries mashed, add a quart and a half of milk-warm water and twelve ounces of good loaf-sugar bruised and dissolved. Stir the whole well in the tub or vat, and throw a blanket over the vessel, which is proper in making all wines, unless you wish to slacken the process of fermentation. Stir the ingredients occasionally, and in three days strain off the liquor into a cask. Keep the cask full, and when the spiritous fermentation has ceased, add, for every gallon of wine a half-pint of brandy or good whisky, and the same quantity of Sherry or Madeira. Bung up the cask very closely, covering the bung with clay; and when fined, which will be in from three to six months, rack it carefully off, and rack it again if not quite bright.

N.B.—The fruit here should be rather over-ripe. A very excellent white-currant wine may be made by this receipt, or a wine of white gooseberries and white currants mixed.

Cook and Housewife's Manual (1829).

CLARET
AN ARTIFICIAL CLARET

The juice of clary, or the water of clary distilled in a cold still, one part; Red-streak, or pippin cider, half a part; Malaga raisins beat in a mortar, six pounds; the fat Mother of Claret, one pound; of the chrystals of tartar half a pound; and being close covered, let it ferment the space of fifteen days, then draw off the liquor clear into a barrel; to every gallon thereof add half a pint of the juice of blackberries or gooseberries and a pint of spirit of clary to the whole; then take three spoonfuls of flour, the white of two new laid eggs, a dram of isinglass, being all beat together, add it into the barrel with two pounds of the syrup of clary, and it will refine down and become wonderful rich.

English Wines (1691).

ENGLISH CLARET

Take six gallons of water, two gallons of cider, and eight pounds of Malaga raisins bruised; put them all together, and let them stand close covered in a warm place for a fortnight, stir it every other day. Then strain the liquor into a clean cask, and put to it a quart of barberries, a pint of the juice of raspberries, and a pint of black cherry juice. Work it up with a little mustard seed, and cover with a piece of dough three or four days by the fire-side; then let it stand a week, and bottle it off. When fine and ripe, it will be like common claret.

Duncan Macdonald, New London Family Cook (c. 1800).

CYPRUS
CYPRUS WINE IMITATED

You must, to nine gallons of water, put nine quarts of the juice of white elder berries which have been pressed gently from the berries with the hand, and passed through a sieve without bruising the kernels of the berries; add to every gallon of liquor, three pounds of Lisbon sugar, and to the whole quantity, put an ounce and an half of ginger sliced, and three quarters of an ounce of cloves, then boil this half an hour, taking off the scum as it rises, and pour the whole in an open tub to cool, and work it with ale yeast, spread upon a toast of white bread, for three days, then turn it into a vessel that will just hold it, adding about a pound and a half of raisins of the sun split, to lie in the liquor till drawn off, which should not be till the wine is fine which you will find in January.

The wine is so much like the fine rich wine brought from Cyprus, in its colour and flavour, that it has deceived the best judges.

The British Jewel (1782).

FRONTIGNAC
ENGLISH FRONTIGNAC

Whisk six whites of eggs in six gallons of water, and put to this sixteen pounds of good loaf-sugar. Boil and skim it well. Put to the boiling liquid eight pounds of the best raisins chopped, and a quarter-peck of elderflowers. Infuse these, but do not boil them. When cool, put a quarter-pint of yeast to the liquid, stirring it well up. Next day put in the juice of four lemons and the thin rind. Let it ferment in the open vessel for three days, and then strain and cask it.

Obs. This wine, if properly managed, resembles Frontignac.
Cook and Housewife's Manual (1829).

TO MAKE FRONTINIAC-WINE

Take six gallons of water, twelve pounds of white sugar, and six pounds of raisins of the sun cut small; boil these together an hour; then take of the flowers of elder, when these are falling, and will shake off, the quantity of half a peck; put them in the liquor when it is almost cold; the next day put in six spoonfuls of syrup of lemon, and four spoonfuls of ale-yeast, and two days after put it in a vessel that is fit for it; and when it has stood two months, bottle it off.
Gilleroy (1762).

MADEIRA
MOCK MADEIRA OR MALTA WINE

Take 30 lb. of coarse sugar and 10 gallons of water (wine measure) and boil it half an hour, take the scum clean off and when it has stood till it is as warm as new milk, put to every gallon one quart of new ale from the vat. Let it work in the tub a day or two then put it in the barrel with one pound of brown sugar candy pounded, 4 lb. of raisins and 2 ounces of isinglass. When it has done working put to it one quart of brandy and stop it close. Let it stand one year in the cask, then bottle it off and the longer it stands in the bottles before you drink it the better the wine will be.
MS. Book of Recipes (early nineteenth century).

TO MAKE BRITISH MADEIRA

To a gallon of water, put three pounds of Lisbon sugar; boil it together twenty minutes, and make it quite clear from scum; when cold, to every gallon, add one pound of Smyrna raisins, chopped, and a quart of new ale; when working in the vat, tun it together, and let it stand in the cask for six months, then bottle it.

Addison Ashburn (1807).

BRITISH MADEIRA
Put a bushel of pale malt into a tub, and pour on it eleven gallons of boiling water, after stirring them together, cover the vessel over, and let them stand to infuse for three hours: strain the liquor through a sieve, dissolve it in three pounds and a half of sugar candy, and ferment it with yeast in the usual manner. After fermenting three days (during which time the yeast is to be skimmed off three or four times a day) pour the clear liquor into a clean cask, and add the following articles mixed together : French brandy, two quarts; raisin wine, five pints; and red port, two bottles : stir them together, and let the cask be well bunged and kept in a cool place for ten months, when it will be fit to bottle. After having been kept in the bottle twelve months, it will be found not inferior to East-India Madeira. Good table-beer may be made with the malt after it has been infused for making this wine.

Anthony Haselmore (1823).

MALAGA
AN ARTIFICIAL MALAGA WINE
First take a wine-barrel hooped and dressed with one end being open, to which a close cover must be fitted, which must take off and put on at pleasure, set it in a warm place winter or summer, and fill it full with clear and pure water, to each three gallons put six pounds of the best Malaga raisins, which you must bruise in a stone mortar, and upon twenty gallons of the said water you must strew a handfull of *calxvive;* then cover the vessel close with the cover, and cast cloths upon it to keep it warm, and let it stand four or five days, to work as wine or beer does, when they are new; then see if the raisins have risen up to the top of the water, if so, then put them down again, as before; let them thus stand three weeks or a month together with the raisins, every fourth or fifth day put down if they raise up; then put a tap into the vessel three or four fingers above the bottom, and try if it be good, and tastes like wine; if not let it stand a while longer; but if so, draw it off into another wine

vessel, and to every twenty gallons that you have drawn off, put a pint of the best *aquavitæ*, two new laid eggs, and a quart of *alligant* beaten well together, and let stand in a cellar as other wine does, till it be clear and fit to be drunk, and thus not only artificial Malaga may be made, but also other artificial wines; for the author cannot but presuppose that you can by these examples invent and prepare other sorts of wines, which are not here set down, by the same method as that of muscadine is prepared; for having the knowledge of the different herbs that bear a signature with the different sulphurs of the true wine, whether stiptic, acid, mild, pleasant, luscious, or fat and balsamic, so must the imitation of the different sort of wines be, whether Rapadavia, Ribella, Canary, Tent, or any other.

English Wines (1691).

ENGLISH MOUNTAIN

Pick out all the large stalks of some Malaga raisins; chop them very small, and put five pounds to every gallon of cold spring water. Let them remain a fortnight or more, then squeeze out the liquor, and put it into a proper cask, after having been fumigated with a match. Let it remain unstopped till the hissing or fermentation has ceased; then bung it up, and, when fine, bottle it off.

Duncan Macdonald, New London Family Cook (c. 1800).

MARSALA
TO MAKE PALERMO WINE

Take to every quart of water a pound of Malaga raisins, rub and cut the raisins small, and put them to the water, and let them stand ten days, stirring once or twice a day; you may boil the water an hour before you put it to the raisins, and let stand to cool; at ten days end strain out your liquor, and put a little yeast to it; and at three days end put it in the vessel, with one sprig of dried wormwood; let it be close stopped, and at three months' end bottle it off.

Gelleroy—London Cook (1764).

PORT
ENGLISH PORT

Put eight gallons of good port into a sixty-gallon cask, first fumed with a match; add to it forty gallons of good cider, and fill the hogshead with French brandy. The juice of elderberries and sloes will give it the proper roughness, and cochineal will colour it.

Turnip juice, or raisin cider, may be used instead of cider, and British spirits instead of French brandy.

Duncan Macdonald, New London Family Cook (c. 1800).

TO MAKE BRITISH PORT

To six gallons of water, put six quarts of elderberries, when quite ripe, and three quarts of blackberries, and six quarts of damsons; boil them all together for three-quarters of an hour; then strain it through a hair sieve, and put to it twelve pounds of loaf sugar, and still it till the sugar is dissolved; when the liquor is near cold, add some new yeast, and let it stand till the next day; then tun it into the vessel, with fifteen pounds of raisins chopped small, and one gallon of sloes, baked; stop it close, and let it stand in the barrel twelve months, then bottle it.

N.B.—The longer it is kept, the better it will prove.

Addison Ashburn (1807).

BRITISH PORT

Take of grape wine, or good cider, four gallons; fresh juice of red elder berries, one gallon; brandy, two quarts; logwood, four ounces; rhatany root (bruised), half a pound. Infuse the logwood and rhatany root in the brandy, and a gallon of the grape wine or cider, for a week; then strain off the liquor, and mix it with the other ingredients. Keep it in a cask well bunged for a month, when it will be fit to bottle.

The New London Cookery (1823).

RHENISH
BRITISH RHENISH

To every gallon of fresh apple-juice, add two pounds of loaf sugar. Boil and skim this till quite limpid. Strain it. Ferment it as other wines; and when the head flattens, rack it off clear and tun it. Next season rack it off again; add a pint of brandy to every three gallons.

Obs. This is a highly-reputed wine, but we have no actual experience of its qualities.

Cook and Housewife's Manual (1829).

114

TO MAKE SARAGOSSA WINE OR ENGLISH SACK

To every quart of water put a sprig of rue, and to every gallon a handful of fennel roots; boil these half an hour, then strain it out, and to every gallon of this liquor put three pounds of honey, boil it two hours, and skim it well; when it is cold, pour it off, and turn it into the vessel, or such cask as is fit for it; keep it a year in the vessel, and then bottle it; it is a very good sack.

Gelleroy—London Cook (1762).

SHERRY
ENGLISH SHERRY

Boil 30 lb. of sugar in 10 gallons of water and scum it clear. When cold put a quart of new ale-wort to every gallon of liquor, and let it work in the tub a day or two. Then put it in the cask with a pound of sugar candy, six pounds of fine raisins, a pint of brandy, and two ounces of isinglass. When the fermentation is over, stop it close; let it stand eight months, rack it off and add a little more brandy. Put it in the cask again, and let it stand four months before it is bottled.

The New Female Instructor.

ENGLISH SHERRY

To every pound of good moist sugar, put one quart of water. Boil it till it is clear; when cool (as near as possible to cold without being quite so) work it with new yeast, and add of strong beer in the height of working, the proportion of one quart in a gallon. Cover it up, and let it work the same as beer; when the fermentation begins to subside, tun it; and when it has been in the cask a fortnight or three weeks, add raisins, half a pound to a gallon, sugar candy and bitter almonds of each half an ounce to a gallon, and to nine gallons of wine half a pint of the best brandy. Paste a stiff brown paper over the bung-hole, and if necessary renew it. For all British wines, brown paper thus pasted on is preferable to a bung. This wine will be fit to bottle after remaining one year in the cask; but if left longer will be improved. If suffered to remain three years in the cask and one in bottles, it can scarcely be distinguished from good foreign wines, and for almost every purpose answers exactly as well.

The New London Cookery (c. 1827).

MEAD AND METHEGLIN

Long before the vine and the true Faith were brought to these shores, before even the Romans had taught the Britons the rudiments of agriculture and how to brew ale from grain, a form of native "wine" was made, a honey wine, of which the alcohol was obtained through the fermentation of honey: it was called mead. Mead, the honey drink, is probably as old as wine, the wine from grapes, and its appeal must have been as universal, in the beginning, since mead, like wine, can easily be recognised in a number of ancient languages : *Methu* means honey, in Greek; *Madhu* has the same meaning in Sanscrit; *Miod* is the honey-drink in Danish; it is *Medu* in Saxon, and *Medd* in Welsh, hence *Metheglin*, from *Medd*, mead, and *Llyn*, liquor. Mead and Metheglin lost much of their former popularity in Britain when ale and wine became their rivals, but never ceased to be brewed and are still made even now.

Mead used to be drunk out of mead-horns, the most intemperate of drinking vessels, since one was obliged, thirsty or not, to drain it to the last drop before one could lay it down. In the course of time, mead and metheglin, sometimes called mead-wine, became more and more complicated in the making, as will be seen from the following recipes from manuscript books of family recipes and printed books, some old and others of recent date.

TO MAKE MEATH

Take to every gallon of water, a quart of honey, and set it over a clear fire, and when it is ready to boil, skim it very clear. Then take two handfulls of sweet-marjoram, as much rosemary, and as much balm : and two handfulls of fennel-roots, as much of parsley-roots, and as many asparagus-roots : slice them in the middle, and take out the pith, wash and scrape them very clean, and put them with your herbs into your liquor. Then take two ounces of ginger, one ounce of nutmeg, half an ounce of mace : bruise them and put them in : and let it boil till it be so strong that it will bear an egg : then let it cool : and being cold, put in three or four spoonfulls of new ale-yeast : and so skim it well, and put it into a runlet, and it will work like ale : and having done working, stop it up close, as you do new beer : and lay salt upon it.

Sir Kenelme Digby (1669).

TO MAKE METHEGLIN

Take four gallons of running water, and boil it a quarter of an hour, and put it in an earthen vessel, and let it stand all night. The next day take only the water, and leave the settling at the bottom : so put the honey in a thin bag, and work it in the water, till all the honey is dissolved. Take to four gallons of water, one gallon of honey : then put in an egg. If it be strong enough of the honey, the egg will part of it appear on the top of the liquor : if it do not, put more honey to it till it do. Then take out the egg, and let the liquor stand till next morning. Then take two ounces of ginger, and slice it and pare it; some rosemary washed and stripped from the stalk : dry it very well.

The next day put the rosemary and ginger into the drink, and so set it on the fire : when it is almost ready to boil, take the whites of three eggs well beaten with the shells, and put all into the liquor : and stir it about and skim it well till it be clear. Be sure you skim not off the rosemary and ginger : then take it off the fire, and let it run through a hair sieve : and when you have strained it, pick out the rosemary and ginger out of the strainer, and put it into the drink, and throw away the eggshells, and so let it stand all night. The next day tun it up in a barrel : be sure the barrel be not too big : then take a little flour and a little bran and the white of an egg, and beat them well together, and put them into the barrel on the top of the metheglin, after it hath done working; then stop it up as close as is possible : and so let it stand till it has done working; then stop it up as close as is possible : and so let it stand six or seven weeks : then draw it out and bottle it. You must tie down the corks, and set the bottles in sand five or six weeks, and then drink it.

Sir Kenelme Digby (1669).

TO MAKE METHEGLIN THAT LOOKS LIKE WHITE WINE

Take to twelve gallons of water, a handful of each of these herbs: parsley, eglantine, rosemary, strawberry-leaves, wild-thyme, balm, liver-wort, betony, scabious : when the water begins to boil, cast in the herbs : let them boil a quarter of an hour : then strain out the herbs; and when it is almost cold, then put in as much of the best honey you can get as will bear an egg to the breadth of two pence; that is, till you can see no more of the egg above the water than two pence will cover. Lave it and stir it till you see all the honey be melted; then boil it well half an hour, at the least : skim it well, and put in the whites of six eggs beaten, to clarify it : then strain it into some wooden vessels and when it is almost cold, put some ale-barm into it. And when it worketh well, tun it into some well-seasoned vessel, where neither ale nor beer has been, for marring the colour of it.

When it has done working, if you like it, take a quantity of cloves, nutmegs, mace, cinnamon, ginger, or any of these that you like best, and bruise them, and put them in a boulter bag, and hang it in the vessel. Put not too much of the spice, because many do not like the taste of much spice. If you make it at Michaelmas, you may tap it at Christmas : but if you keep it longer, it will be the better. It will look pure, and drink with as much spirit as can be, and very pleasant.

Sir Kenelme Digby (1669).

MEATH OR HYDROMEL

Meath or hydromel is of two sorts, the weaker and the stronger meath or metheglin.

If your mead be not strong enough by the refuse of your combs, then put so much of your coarse honey into it, as will make it strong enough to bear an egg the breadth of a two-pence above the top of the liquor, which is sufficient for ordinary mead, and afterwards till night, ever and anon stir it about the kive. If you would make a greater quantity, then you must add a greater measure of water and honey, namely six gallons of water to one of honey; some will boil this proportion of six to one, to four, but I think to five is very sufficient, the spices to this proportion are cinnamon, ginger, pepper, grains of paradise, cloves of each two drams. The next morning put to the liquor some of the scum of the honey; stir them together, and stoop the kive a little backwards, when it hath settled an hour or two draw it off to be boiled, and when you see the sediment appear, stop, and let the rest run into some vessel by itself, which, when settled strain into the boiler, and the dregs of all cast into your garden for the use of your bees.

When your liquor is set over a gentle fire, and a thick scum is gathered all over, and the bubbles by the sides begin to break the scum; having damped your fire to cease the boiling, skim it clean, and then presently blow up your fire; and when you see the second scum ready, having again damped the fire, take off the scum as before, and then having again stirred your fire let it boil handsomely for the space of an hour, or thereabouts, but be sure you always keep scumming it as there is occasion.

After all this is done, put in your spices according to the former receipt, and let it boil a quarter of an hour more at least: the end of boiling is to cleanse the mead, which once done any farther boiling does but rather diminish than increase the goodness and strength of the mead.

As soon as it has done boiling take it from the fire and set it to cool; the next day when it is settled, strain it through a hair sieve, or linen bag, into the kive, reserving still the dregs for the bees, and let it stand covered three or four days till it work, and let it work two days, then turn it into a barrel scalded with bay leaves, making the spicebag fast at the tap. If you make no great quantity of mead, you may tun it the next day and let it work in the barrel; your ordinary mead which turns sour will make excellent good vinegar.

Metheglin is the more generous and stronger sort of hydromel, for it beareth an egg to the breadth of six pence and is usually made of finer honey with a less proportion of water, namely of four to one. To every barrel of sixteen gallons of skimmed liquor, add thyme one ounce, eglantine, sweet marjoram of each half an ounce, ginger two ounces, cinnamon one ounce, cloves and pepper of each half an ounce; all gross beaten, the one half boiled loose in the liquor, and the other half put in a bag as before in mead; so that after this manner being made an ordinary mead will not keep above half a year; this, the longer it is kept, the stronger it is, and hath the more delicate flavour and taste.

This was a drink frequently used amongst the ancient Romans who, I suppose, first taught the ordering of bees, and brought this wholesome liquor into our island. We find by history it was the approved and common drink of our ancestors, even of our kings and queens, who, in former ages, preferred the liquors of the product of this island, before those imported from foreign countries, as did the famous Queen Elizabeth, who every year had a vessel of metheglin made for her own drinking; a receipt of which take as follows.

Take a bushel of sweet briar leaves, as much of thyme, half a bushel of rosemary leaves, and a peck of bay leaves and having well washed them, boil them in a copper of fair water, let them boil the space of half an hour or better, and then pour out all the water and herbs into a vat, and let it stand till it be but milk-warm, then strain the water from the herbs, and take to every gallon of water, one gallon of the finest honey, and beat it together for the space of an hour, and let it stand two days, stirring it well twice or thrice a day; then take the liquor and boil it again, and skim it as long as there remains any scum, when it is clear put it into a vat as before, and let it stand to cool. You must then have in readiness a kive of new ale or beer, which as soon as you have emptied suddenly put in the metheglin, and let it stand three days working, and then tun it up in barrels, tying at every tap-hole by a packthread, a little bag of beaten cloves and mace to the value of an ounce. It must stand half a year before it be drank.

England's Interest (1721).

TO MAKE MEAD

Put to 18 gallons of water 27 lb. of honey. Set it to boil, scum it as long as any rises, put in 4 nutmegs sliced, 24 cloves, and the peel of 2 or 3 lemons. Let it boil in all 2 hours at least. Set it to cool and when it is blood warm set it working with a quart of ale-yeast. Let it work half a day. Tun it up but before you stop it let it come to a head. After a week or ten days bottle it.

D. L. MS. (dated 1727).

TO MAKE STRONG MEAD

Take of spring water what quantity you please, make it more then blood-warm, and dissolve honey in it till it is strong enough to bear an egg the breadth of a shilling, then boil it gently, near an hour, taking off the scum as it rises; then put to about nine or ten gallons, seven or eight large blades of mace, three nutmegs quartered, twenty cloves, three or four sticks of cinnamon, two or three roots of ginger, and a quarter of an ounce of Jamaica pepper; put these spices into the kettle to the honey and water, a whole lemon, with a sprig of sweet-briar, and a sprig of rosemary; tie the briar and rosemary together, and when they have boiled a little while, take them out and throw them away; but let your liquor stand on the spice in a clean earthen pot, till the next day; then strain it into a vessel that is fit for it, put the spice in a bag, hang it in the vessel, stop it, and at three months draw it into bottles; be sure that it is fine when it is bottled; after it is bottled six weeks, it is fit to drink.

Gelleroy—London Cook (1762)

A RECEIPT FOR WHITE MEAD WINE

To every gallon of water, put a pint of honey, and one pound of loaf sugar; stir in the white of six eggs, beat to a froth, and boil it as long as any scum arises. When it is cold work it with yeast, and to every gallon put the peel of three large lemons, thin sliced, and also the juice strained through a cloth. Stop it up when done working, and bottle it in ten days.

Daily Companion (1799).

TO MAKE MEAD

To every gallon of water, put four pounds of honey; when your water is warm put in your honey, and keep stirring it till it boils; scum it well, and let it boil half an hour; to fifteen gallons, put two ounces of hops; let them boil in it, in a bag; when cold put it in the vessel, and stop it up directly. Let it stand a year in the barrel, then bottle it.

Addison Ashburn (1807).

TO MAKE COWSLIP MEAD

To fifteen gallons of water put thirty pounds of honey, boil it till one gallon is wasted, scum it, then take it off the fire, have ready sixteen lemons cut in halves, take a gallon of the

121

liquor, and put it to the lemons, put the rest of the liquor into a tub, with seven pecks of cowslips, and let them stand all night, then put in the liquor with the lemons, and eight spoonfuls of new yeast, a handful of sweet briar, stir them all well together, and let it work three or four days, then strain it, and put it in your cask, and in six months time you may bottle it.

English Housekeeper (1806).

TO MAKE WALNUT MEAD

To every gallon of water put three pounds and a half of honey, boil them together three quarters of an hour, to every gallon of liquor put about two dozen of walnut leaves, pour your liquor boiling hot upon them, let them stand all night, then take the leaves out and put in a spoonful of yeast, and let it work two or three days, then make it up, and let it stand three months, then bottle it.

English Housekeeper (1806).

BARLEY MEAD

Take the juice of four limes, the rind pared thin of two, four tablespoonfuls of honey and half a pound of pearl barley; put it into a jug or other vessel, and pour two quarts of boiling water upon it; let it stand to cool and strain it.

Indian Domestic Economy (1849).

MEAD WINE

There are different kinds of this wine; but those generally made are two, namely, sack-mead and cowslip-mead. Sack-mead is made thus : To every gallon of water put four pounds of honey, and boil it three quarters of an hour, taking care properly to skim it. To each gallon add half an ounce of hops then boil it half an hour, and let it stand till next day. Then put it into your cask; and to thirteen gallons of the liquor add a quart of brandy or sack. Let it be lightly closed till the fermentation is over, and then stop it up very close. If you make as much as fills a large cask, you must not bottle it off till it has stood a year.

To make cowslip-mead, you must proceed thus : Put thirty pounds of honey into fifteen gallons of water, and boil it till one gallon is wasted; skim it, take it off the fire, and have ready sixteen lemons cut in half. Take a gallon of the liquor and

put it to the lemons. Pour the rest of the liquor into a tub, with seven pecks of cowslips, and let them stand all night, then put in the liquor with the lemons, eight spoonfuls of new yeast, and a handful of sweet-briar; stir all well together, and let it work three or four days. Then strain it, pour it into your cask, let it stand six months, and then bottle it off for use.
Female Instructor (1812).

MEAD WINE (SECOND)

The article now before us, was obtained from a lady in the country, who has always been particularly attached to mead wine, and whose manner of making it we shall give in her own words : "To one hundred and twenty gallons of pure water, the softer the better, I put fifteen gallons of clarified honey. When the honey is well mixed with the water, I fill my copper, the same as I use for brewing, which only holds sixty gallons, and boil it till it is reduced about a fourth part. I then draw it off, and boil the remainder of the liquor in the same manner. When this last is about a fourth part wasted, I fill up the copper with some of that which was first boiled, and continue boiling and filling it up, till the copper contains the whole of the liquor, by which time it will of course be half evaporated. I must observe that in boiling I never take off the scum, but on the contrary have it well mixed with the liquor whilst boiling, by means of a jet.

"When this is done, I draw it off into underbacks, by a cock at the bottom of the copper, in which I let it remain till it is only as warm as new milk. At this time I tun it, and suffer it to ferment in the vessel, where it will form a thick head. As soon as it has done working, I stop it down very close, in order to keep the air from it as much as possible. I keep this, as well as my mead, in a cellar or vault I have for the purpose, being very deep and cool, and the door shut so close, as to keep out, in a manner, all the outward air, so that the liquor is always in the same temperature, being not at all affected by the change of weather. To this I attribute, in a great measure, the goodness of my mead.

"Another proportion I have of making mead, is to allow eighty pounds of clarified honey to one hundred and twenty gallons of soft water, which I manage in the making in all respects like the before mentioned, and it proves very pleasant, good light drinking; and is, by many, preferred to the other, which is much richer, and has a fuller flavour; but at the same time it is more inebriating, and apt to make the head ache, if drank in too large quantities. I imagine therefore, upon the whole, the last to be the proportion that makes the wholesomest liquor for common drink, the other being rather, when properly preserved, a rich cordial, something like fine old Malaga, which, when in perfection, is justly esteemed the best of the Spanish wines.

"I choose, in general, to have the liquor pure and genuine, though many like it best when it has an aromatic flavour, and for this purpose they mix elder, rosemary, and marjoram flowers with it; and also use cinnamon, cloves, ginger, and cardamoms, in various proportions, according to their taste : But I do not approve of this last practice at all, as green herbs are apt to make the mead drink flat; and too many cloves, besides being very predominant in the taste, make it of too high a colour. I never bottle mead before it is half a year old, and when I do, I take care to have it well corked, and keep it in the same vault wherein it stood whilst in cask."

Female Instructor (1812).

MEAD

To every gallon of water put four pounds of honey; boil it an hour; then put it into a tub with some yeast on a toast, cover it over. If it ferments well, after three or four days draw it off clear, put it into a cask with one lemon sliced to every gallon, add a bottle of brandy to every ten gallons. The rind of Seville oranges cut very thin, suspended in the barrel, will greatly improve the flavour. It is best to wash the cask round with part of the brandy before the liquor is put in. Those who like mead to have an aromatic flavour may mix with it elder, rosemary, marjoram flowers and use cinnamon, cloves, ginger, pepper, and cardamums in various proportions, according to taste. Others put in a mixture of thyme, eglantine, rosemary, marjoram, with various spices.

Bishop (1860).

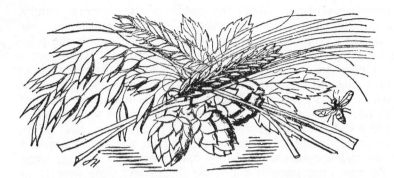

ALE AND BEER

Ale is the most lasting legacy left behind them by the Romans when they finally quitted Britain. They taught the natives how to till the land, how to grow grain, and how to make an alcoholic drink from barley, corn, oats or millet. The art of brewing attained a high degree of perfection from a very early age, since we find the following description of the process in a manuscript of the fifth century: "The grain is steeped in water, and made to germinate: it is then dried and ground; after which it is infused in a certain quantity of water, which, being fermented, becomes a pleasant, warming, strengthening, intoxicating liquor."

Of course, at the time and long after, there was no mention of hops: hops came in with the Reformation, in King Henry the Eighth's reign. Ale was not made by brewers only, at first, but mostly by every householder for household consumption: but its making and sale were regulated as early as the seventh century, by Ina, King of Wessex, who ascended the throne in or about the year 689.

Ale was the favourite drink of Anglo-Saxons and Danes: it was the common drink of all, and not merely of the common people, being served at all royal and noble feasts before wine, and it was sold to all and sundry, at all times of the day and night, in beer-houses, the entry to which was denied to priests, but no one else.

Long before hops were used in the brewing of ale, spices were used to add flavour as well as for the sake of avoiding or retarding souring. About the middle of the eleventh century, at a royal banquet presided over by Edward the Confessor, the best ale served cost 8*d*. per gallon, which was double the price of common ale, that is, ale which was spiced.

Under the Plantagenets, when the whole of the vineyards of Guyenne and Gascony were part of the English realm, beverage wines were so cheap, in England, as to be within the reach of all but the poorest in the land; their consumption was enormous, but it did not affect in any degree the popularity of ale. Thus, in 1256, during the reign of Henry III, the brewers were a very rich corporation, and they have remained thus ever since. the maximum price at which ale, bread and wine were to be sold was fixed by authority during many centuries, by the King's authority at first, and later by Parliament. Originally, however, the licensed brewers were all women, or ale-wives, and in all the large households, where ale continued to be brewed for the family's use as late as the nineteenth century, it was usually either the lady of the house or one of her trusted maids who was responsible for brewing the ale.

Hops were used by the brewers of the Netherlands as early as the fourteenth century, but they were not finally accepted in England until some two hundred years later. Henry VI forbade the planting of hops, and Henry VIII forbade the brewers to put either sulphur or hops in their ale, but Edward VI granted licences for the planting of hop-grounds and hops claimed more and more of the soil of England from that time.

According to Johnson's Dictionary, ale was "A liquor brewed from malt, to be drunk fresh." This used to be known as common ale, in opposition to spiced ale, which used to be flavoured with a number of spices and herbs, other than hops. Hopped ale was called beer, and was meant to be matured. Since the nineteenth century, however, whatever differences there may be between ale and beer are due to purely local tradition in various parts of the country. According to the Shorter Oxford English Dictionary, ale and beer were originally synonymous; but now "beer" is the generic name for all malt liquors, "ale" being the name for the lighter coloured kinds. This is wrong; hops made all the difference originally between ale and beer, and there are now ales just as dark as the darkest beer, other than stout. When ale is stale it is often called beery, probably owing to a survival of the tradition that ale was best freshly brewed, not having, like beer, the benefit of hops, chiefly used originally as a preservative.

Beer is the most popular thirst-quenching beverage in all lands where there are no vineyards, and where wine is accordingly too dear for most people for daily use. Beer is fermented from malted barley, hopped and filtered, or fined, before being drunk. The taste, flavour and gravity (or alcoholic strength) of beer depend upon the quality of the malt and that of the water used, in the first instance; then upon the manner and method of brewing, bottling and keeping.

Malt is obtained by wetting and spreading barley on a floor, allowing it to germinate, when it is dried in a kiln. The method of drying the malt has much to do with the colour of the beer.

The malt is then ground in a mill and becomes grist; the grist and plenty of hot water are mixed in a tub and become the mash, in the mash tub; hops are put in, the wort is extracted from the mash and boiled with it, then cooled. The wort passes on into the fermenting tank. Yeast is then added and fermentation sets in; it produces carbonic acid gas, which loses itself in the air, and alcohol, which remains in what was the wort and now becomes beer. Beer is then racked into casks or fined and bottled, each brewer having his own method for fining, filtering, sweetening or not, dry-hopping or not, and otherwise giving the last "finishing touch" to the beer he is going to sell.

The strength of the beer, of course, depends upon the proportion of water to malt; the more malt the greater the strength; the more water the milder the beer. The result of the late Mr. A. Chaston Chapman's analysis of a number of London and country brews of beer shows great differences in the strength of pre-war beers :—

Alcoholic content % by weight

Type of beer			London	Country
Strong ale and old ale	..	..	8.43	5.36
Bitter and pale ale	..	..	3.92	3.62
Stout and porter	..	..	3.75	3.45
			English	Foreign
Lager ..	..	..	4.03	3.54
Mild ale and table beer	..	..	3.09	3.33

DIRECTIONS FOR BREWING BEER AT HOME

Take 6 gallons of water, 1 peck of malt, 4 ounces of hops. Put the 6 gallons of water into a boiler, while it is coming to the boil scald a wooden tub that will hold 6 gallons and leave plenty of room to stir the beer; it must be very clean, and it will be found a good plan to set it full of water overnight to be quite sure it will not leak.

When the water boils, pour it into the tub, let it stand 6 minutes, then put in the malt, stir it well, and cover it close with sacks; let it stand 3 days and 3 nights near the fire so that it keeps warm. Now strain it from the malt, put it into the boiler with the hops, boil these together quickly for $\frac{1}{2}$ hour, strain off at once, and let it cool as quickly as possible.

When only milk warm, put in $1\frac{1}{2}$ teacupfuls of yeast; let it ferment for 2 days; it must be skimmed frequently, and the skimmings will be as much as 3 pints or 2 quarts of good yeast. Then put it into a cask, taking care that it is clean and sweet; leave the bung out for a few hours, to be quite sure the fermentation is over, stop it down close, and put the cask into an underground cellar. This beer is ready to drink in a few weeks.

For a larger brew, take 30 gallons of water, 2 bushels of malt, 2 lb. of hops, and $1\frac{1}{2}$ pints of yeast. Follow the directions given in the other recipe in every particular. A good small beer for the harvest field after this brew is drawn off, with 15 gallons of water, going through the whole process. All that is required is just half the quantity of fresh yeast to finish off.

From Elizabeth Sulley's MS. Book of Recipes (1727).

ALE WITH HONEY

Sir Thomas Gower makes his pleasant and wholesome drink of ale and honey thus : Take forty gallons of small ale, and five gallons of honey. When the ale is ready to tun, and is still warm, take out ten gallons of it; which, while it is hot, mingle with it the five gallons of honey, stirring it exceeding well with a clean arm till they be perfectly incorporated. Then cover it, and let it cool and stand still. At the same time you begin to dissolve the honey in this parcel, you take the other of thirty gallons also warm, and tun it up with barm, and put it into a vessel capable to hold all the whole quantity of ale and honey, and let it work there; and because the vessel will be so far from being full, that the gross foulness of the ale cannot work over, make holes in the sides of the barrel even with the superficies of the liquor in it, out of which the gross seculence may purge; and these holes must be fast shut; when you put in the rest of the ale with the honey; which you must do, when you see the strong working of the other is over: and that it works but gently, which may be after two or three or four days, according to the warmth of the season.

You must warm your solution of honey, when you put it in, to be as warm as ale when you tun it; and then it will set the whole working afresh, and casting out more foulness; which it would do too violently if you put it in at the first of the tunning it. It is not amiss that some seculence lie thick upon the ale, and work not all out; for that will keep in the spirits. After you have dissolved the honey in ale, you must boil it a little to skim it; but skim it not, till it has stood a while from the fire to cool; else you will skim away much of the honey, which will still rise as long as it boils. If you will not make so great a quantity at a time, do it in less in the same proportions.

He makes it about Michaelmas for Lent.

When the strong beer grows too hard and flat for want of spirits, take four or five gallons of it out of a hogshead, and boil five pounds of honey in it, and skim it, and put it warm into the beer; and after it has done working, stop it up close. This will make it quick, pleasant and stronger.

Sir Kenelme Digby (1669).

TO MAKE COCK ALE
Take ten gallons of ale and a large cock, the older the better; parboil the cock, flay him and stamp him in a stone mortar till his bones are broken (you must craw him and gut him when you flay him); then put the cock into two quarts of sack, and put to it three pounds of raisins of the sun stoned, some blades of mace, and a few cloves; put all these into a canvas bag, and a little before you find the ale has done working, put the ale and bag together into a vessel; in a week or nine days' time bottle it up; fill the bottle but just above the neck, and give the same time to ripen as other ale.

Gelleroy—London Cook (1762).

WHITE SPRUCE BEER
To five gallons of water put seven pounds of loaf-sugar,

and three-fourths of a pound of the essence of spruce. Boil
and skim this. Put it into a vessel, and when nearly cool, add
fresh yeast (about half a pint or less). When the beer has
fermented for three days, bung the cask, and in a week bottle.
N.B.—For brown spruce use treacle or coarse brown sugar,
instead of loaf-sugar.

Cook and Housewife's Manual (1829).

TREACLE BEER, A TABLE BEER

Boil, for twenty minutes, three pounds of molasses, in from
six to eight gallons of soft water, with a handful of hops tied
in a muslin bag, or a little extract of gentian. When cooled
in the tub, add a pint of good beer-yeast, or from four to six
quarts of fresh worts from the brewer's vat. Cover the beer
(and all fermenting liquids) with blankets or coarse cloths.
Pour it from the lees and bottle it. You may use sugar for
molasses, which is lighter.

N.B.—This is a cheap and very wholesome beverage. A little
ginger may be added to the boiling liquid if the flavour is liked.

Cook and Housewife's Manual (1829).

TO MAKE WELCH ALE

Pour forty-five gallons of hot water, but not quite boiling,
upon eight bushels of malt; cover, and let it stand three hours.
Meanwhile, infuse four pounds of hops in a little water, and
put the same into the tub, run the wort upon them, and boil
them three hours. Strain off the hops, and keep them for the
small beer. Let the wort stand in a high tub till cool enough
for the yeast, of which, whether of ale or that of small beer,
put in two quarts. Mix the whole thoroughly and stir it often.
When the wort has done fermenting, which will be about the
second or third day, the yeast will sink rather than rise; and
must be removed immediately, and the ale tunned as fast as
it works out. Pour a quart in at a time, but gently, to prevent
the fermentation from continuing too long. Lay some paper
over the bung-hole two or three days previous to stopping it up.

The New London Cookery (1827).

CARROT ALE

Take of water twelve gallons, carrots twenty-four pounds,
treacle four pounds, bran two pounds, dried buck-bean four

ounces and yeast a quarter of a pint. Cut the carrots into thin slices, boil them in the water for an hour (making up the waste in boiling by the addition of a little water), strain it, mash up the bran with the carrot water, stir it well to prevent its clotting, add the treacle, let it stand for half an hour, strain and boil the strained liquor for a quarter of an hour with the buck-bean. Finally strain it, and set aside to cool; when of a sufficient temperature add the yeast, and tun as you would malt beer. This will be found an agreeable and cheap beverage. The cost of the above quantity will be about 3s. 6d.

The New London Cookery (c. 1827).

CHINA ALE

To six gallons of ale made of malt, add a quarter of a pound of China root, thinly sliced, and the same quantity of coriander seeds bruised; hang these in a tiffany or coarse linen bag in the vessel till it has done working, and let it stand a fortnight before it is bottled.

The New London Cookery (c. 1827).

COOL TANKARD

Take a bottle of good ale or porter; put into a covered jug the juice of two limes, part of the peel cut thin, a glass of white wine and some grated nutmeg, enough syrup to sweeten it, a handful of fresh mint or a leaf or two of borrage; pour upon this a pint of water, and put it to cool and stand for fifteen minutes; then add the bottle of beer or porter.

Obs. It may be made at once and drank only adding the beer last.

Indian Domestic Economy (1849).

CIDER

Cider is the fermented juice of apples. It is a very wholesome beverage of great antiquity, and it is made to a large extent in different parts of England, but nowhere in such quantities nor to such perfection as in the West, in Herefordshire, Gloucestershire, Worcestershire, Devonshire and Somerset.

The bad old way, in the good old days, was to fill a circular stone trough with apples, to which was added a little water—for preference, dirty, stagnant water, which would give a "taste." Then a heavy stone wheel was slowly run over the apples and more apples were added until the whole trough was filled with apple juice and apple pulp. This was then pumped into a large vat, where it fermented for some days, after which the "cider" was drawn into casks, and the remaining pulp was made into cakes, dried, and used as food to fatten pigs. Cider made in such a primitive fashion may be quite good, provided the apples are good. It was still made that way some thirty years ago, and it may still be made like it now in out-of-the-way and out-of-date farms on the Continent.

In England, cider has long been made in a more scientific and less wasteful way. In the large cider factories, the apples are pressed by steam presses, and every particle of their juice is extracted. The apples are brought to a crushing mill, where they are reduced to a kind of pulp, which is pressed in layers by means of steam-driven screws, and all the juice squeezed out of the pulp runs into a tank below. It is then drawn into casks, in which fermentation takes place, the sugar contained in the sweet juice of the apple being converted into alcohol and carbonic acid gas.

In very good years and when none but the right sorts of apples are used, the juice contains more sugar than will be used up by fermentation to produce alcohol, and this excess of natural sugar makes the cider taste sweet. In most years, however, all the sugar of the apple juice is transformed into alcohol, and the cider is quite dry, but it may be sweetened at will to suit the taste of the consumer.

When cider is allowed to ferment thoroughly in casks, all the carbonic acid which is generated by fermentation escapes and loses itself in the air; when it is bottled, at a later date, it is quite still, and such is the condition in which most ciders are drunk. Sparkling cider, however, is increasingly popular, and is mostly made by the introduction of carbon dioxide into still cider.

Cider is a most wholesome drink, particularly so in the spring and summer. It is cooling and refreshing and contains neither the ethers of wine nor the essential oils of grain spirits. According to a medical treatise of the early seventeenth century, cider "is best for hot and dry cholerick bodies, hot livers and melancholy persons." Needless to say, cider may be drunk with impunity by "peaceful bodies" and "cheerful persons," and its use need not debar anyone from the pleasure and benefit of good wine.

In Normandy, where cider is made and drunk on a larger scale than anywhere else in Europe, everybody drinks cider, but all those who can afford it drink wine as well.

TO MAKE CIDER

Take a peck of apples, and slice them, and boil them in a barrel of water, till the third part be wasted; then cool your water as you do for wort, and when it is cold, you must pour the water upon three measures of grown apples. Then draw forth the water at a tap three or four times a day, for three days together. Then press out the liquor, and tun it up, when it has done working, then stop it up close.

Sir Kenelme Digby (1669).

TO MAKE CIDER-ROYAL (MR. HAINS'S WAY)

If you must have it drink more like Canary (says Mr. Hains) or other sacks, you must add more of the spirit, and as much syrup or sweets (the making of which is hereinafter taught) as will best please your palate; and as the proportion of one pint of good spirit to a gallon, will make it as strong as French wine; so one pint and a half will make it full as strong as Spanish wine; and by this means in like manner, perry and the juice of cherries, currants and gooseberries (especially gooseberries) may by adding thereunto their proper spirits, or any other fine spirits, be made wine, as good, strong, wholesome and pleasing as the wines made in the Canaries. I mention other spirits, because upon trial I have observed, that brandy, spirit of wine, grain and other spirits, may be of good effect in this business provided they are drawn fine.

The Family Physitian (1696).

WINE OF APPLES AND PEARS

As for apples, make them first into good cider, by beating and pressing and other orderings as I shall direct, when I come to treat of those sort of liquors, after I have ended this of wines; and to good cider when you have procured it, put the herb *scurlea*, the quintessence of wine, and a little fixed nitre, and to a barrel of this cider, a pound of the syrup of honey; let it work and ferment at spurge-holes in the cask ten days, or till you find it clear and well settled, then draw it of, and it will not be much uncomparable to Rhenish wine in clearness, colour and taste.

To make wine of pears, procure the tartest perry (but by by no means that which is tart by souring or given that way) but such as is naturally so, put into a barrel about five ounces of the juice of the herb clary, and the quintessence of wine, and to every barrel a pound, or pint of the syrup of blackberries, and after fermentation, and refining, it will be of a curious wine-taste like sherry, and not well distinguishable, but by such as have very good palates, or whose trade it is to deal with it.

Their virtues: These wines have the nature of cider and perry, though in a higher degree, by the addition and alteration, being cooling, restorative, easing pains in the liver or spleen, cleansing the bowels, and creating a good appetite.

The Way to get Wealth (1706).

To make cider-royal, or raise ordinary cider to be full as good, or better than French wine; or to make the best simple cider twice as strong as it is (and so the like of any of the aforesaid liquors), is by putting the strength and goodness of two hogsheads into one; which is thus effected:

First: Put one hogshead of cider, and some part of the other, into a copper-still, and draw off all the spirit; after which distil the said spirit a second time, and then put the same into your other hogshead, and fill it up, stir it about well and keep it close stopped, except one day in ten or twenty let it lie open five or six hours. And within one quarter of a year, if the ensuing direction be observed, this cider will be full as strong or stronger than the best French wine, and altogether as pleasing, though it may be somewhat different to taste.

But if you would have it drink more like Canary or other sacks, you must add more of the spirit, and as much sugar or sweets (the making of which is hereinafter taught) as will best please your palate. And as the proportion of one pint of good spirit to a gallon, will make it as strong as French wine, so one pint and a half will make it full as strong as Spanish wine; and by this means, in like manner, perry and the juice of cherries, mulberries, currants, and gooseberries (especially gooseberries) may, by adding thereunto their proper spirits, or any other convenient spirits, be made as good and pleasing as the wines made in the Canaries.

England's Interest (1721).

A RICH AND PLEASANT WINE

Take new cider from the press, mix it with as much honey as will support an egg, boil gently fifteen minutes, but not in an iron, brass or copper pot. Skim it well; when cool, let it be tunned, but don't quite fill. In March following bottle it, and it will be fit to drink in six weeks; but will be less sweet if kept longer in the cask. You will have a rich and strong wine, and it will keep well. This will serve for any culinary purposes which milk, or sweet wine, is directed for.

Honey is a fine ingredient to assist, and render palatable, new crabbed austere cider.

Domestic Cookery (1814).

PUNCH

TO MAKE PUNCH-ROYAL

Two quarts of water, one pound and a half of loaf-sugar, and dissolve it fully therein, and if need be filter it through a Holland cloth, then add a pint of Rhenish wine and 6 ounces of lime-juice, or the juice of four great lemons, and 7 or 8 drops of the true spirit of salt, and a drachm of alkermes, or 2 grains of musk, and 3 of amber grease, a quart of brandy, one nutmeg grated, and stir it till it be incorporated, and then head it with toasted biscuits; this liquor, without bread, drinks exceeding briskly, being bottled for a time.

English Wines (1691).

BOTTLED PUNCH

To one gallon of the best brandy, put the parings of six lemons, and as many oranges, infuse them together for four days. In the meantime take twelve pints of soft water, and one pound and a half of fine sugar, with the whites of six eggs, beaten up to a froth, in a little of the said cold water; mix them together and set the liquor over the fire, and when it boils, scum it clean whilst any thing rises. Then take it from the fire, and when it is fully cold, put it into a proper vessel, and add to it the brandy with the peels, with as much juice of lemons as you think proper. Stop up the vessel close, and let it stand for six weeks, then rack it carefully off for use.

This is a strong punch, to be used only as a cordial dram, of a grateful taste and flavour, and is sold in some taverns under a foreign appellation.

The Practical Distiller (1734).

VERDER, OR MILK PUNCH

Pare six oranges, and six lemons, as thin as you can, grate them after with sugar to get the flavour. Steep the peels in a bottle of rum or brandy close stopped twenty-four hours. Squeeze the fruit on two pounds of sugar, add to it four quarts of water, and one of new milk boiling hot; stir the rum into the above, and run it through a jelly-bag till perfectly clear. Bottle, and cork close immediately.

Domestic Cookery (1814).

NORFOLK PUNCH

Pare thirty-two dozen Seville oranges, and the same number of lemons. Infuse the peel for two days, in a large bottle or jar, with a gallon of brandy (or flavourless whisky), a little reduced in strength. Clarify in a gallon of water, four pounds of sugar. When cold strain the brandy (which will now be a tincture) to this. Add the juice of the oranges and lemons to this; previously strained and bottled, when the peel is taken off. Cask the liquor, or put it in a jar. Stop it well. In six weeks it may be gently poured, or drawn off and bottled. A tincture of bruised nutmegs and cloves may be added to this compound.

Cook and Housewife's Manual (1829).

GLASGOW PUNCH (FROM PETER'S LETTERS)

"The sugar being melted with a little cold water, the artist squeezed about a dozen lemons through a wooden strainer, and then poured in water enough almost to fill the bowl. In this state the liquor goes by the name of sherbet, and a few of the connoisseurs in his immediate neighbourhood were requested to give their opinion of it—for in the mixing of the sherbet lies, according to the Glasgow creed, at least one-half of the whole battle. This being approved by an audible smack from the lips of the umpires, the rum was added to the beverage, I suppose, in something about the proportion of one to seven. Last of all, the maker cut a few limes, and running each section rapidly round the rim of his bowl, squeezed in enough of this most delicate acid to flavour the whole composition. In this consists the true *tour-de-maître* of the punch-maker."

Glasgow punch is made of the coldest spring water newly taken from the spring. The acid ingredients above mentioned will suffice for a very large bowl.

Cook and Housewife's Manual (1829).

"MINERALS" AND SOFT DRINKS

Minerals, to the average man, means rocks and salts, for the average man does not realise that scientists have classed water among the minerals. To the young, however, and to others as well, "minerals" mean "fizzy lemonade," or any form of drink which is gassy, sweet and "soft," by which they mean non-alcoholic. This is the kind of minerals which we propose to deal with in this section.

The name "minerals" was originally given to medicinal waters from "mineral springs"—springs such as those of Bath. Epsom, Buxton and Barnet, in England : the sick went there hopefully to drink their healing waters or bathe in them. All such waters were credited with various curative properties, according to the nature of the various salts, or "minerals," which they contained : hence they were commonly known as mineral waters. Most of them also possessed a distinct liveliness, at the spring, which was for a long time ascribed to their being endowed for a short while with the gift of "life," hence all the more beneficial to ailing persons.

This "sparkling" quality, we know now, is simply due to the fact that such mineral waters are impregnated with carbonic acid gas, and they owe their liveliness to the escape of this gas into the air. But, as late as 1699, Dr. Benjamin Allen, a distinguished man of science, speculating as to the character of the "volatile spirit" present in many of the mineral waters, described it a "vitriolick." Dr. Chrouet, in 1713, when experimenting with spa waters, was the first to express the definite opinion that their effervescing principle was "air and not combustible spirits." In 1741 Dr. Brownrigg demonstrated for the first time the identity of carbonic acid gas in mineral waters; he was also the first to accomplish the artificial aeration of water.

Then, in 1772, Dr. Joseph Priestley, F.R.S., invented and exhibited to the College of Physicians "an apparatus for making aerated water," upon which the College reported favourably. To Priestley is due the credit of the discovery and applications of the principle of charging or saturating water with carbonic acid gas by methods with which we are familiar to-day.

In 1775, a Dr. North invented the gasogene intended to facilitate the more extensive production of aerated waters, and the achievement of a Manchester chemist was admiringly recorded when, thanks to the Gazogene, he succeeded in aerating from 10 to 12 gallons of water in one operation.

So it came to pass that the name of minerals, which had originally been given to the naturally effervescent waters of mineral springs, passed on to artificially carbonated waters entirely free from mineral salts. Nor was it very long before these artificially effervescent waters were made more attractive to the eye and taste by the addition of colouring, sweetening and flavouring matters.

William Francis Hamilton was the first to be granted a patent, in 1809, for "a new method of preparing soda and other mineral waters, spirituous, acetous, saccharine and aromatic liqueurs and sundry improvements relating thereto." But it was not until 1837, when the first syphon was introduced, that aerated waters were bottled in a container which would deliver a portion of its contents, when and as required. Until then, mineral waters had been bottled exclusively in small bulbous, or egg-shaped glass or earthenware containers which could not very well be corked down again once the original cork had been removed.

In 1843, however, glass and earthenware stoppers and screw stoppers made of earthenware were introduced, and they replaced the cork kept in position by a double thread of string. Cadd's patent, which followed, and has now been superseded, had a long run of popularity. Its principle was that the pressure of carbonic acid gas from the "charged" liquid forced a glass ball against a rubber ring inserted in a groove of the specially constructed bottle neck, thus effectively preventing the escape of both liquid and gas until the glass ball was pressed down from outside into a ridge of glass at the base of the bottle neck.

The most usual form of corking minerals to-day is a thin metal disc with crimped edges, lined with cork, which is clamped to the bottle neck by external mechanical pressure; it is known as the "Crown Cork," and it is a most effective, hygienic and inexpensive form of keeping the liquid and its gas within the bottle.*

All "minerals" and what are variously known as temperance drinks, non-alcoholic beverages, or soft drinks, have one feature in common: it is their artificiality—none of them are entirely natural, like grape-juice, orange-juice, or any other freshly pressed fruit juice; nor is any one of them merely one degree or two removed from the original natural state, either by the natural process of fermentation, as in the case of wine and cider, or by the same process of fermentation, following upon the germination or malting of the grain, in the case of beer.

In all ripe fruit, as in all else in nature, there is harmony without monotony; there are two partners, entirely different, but not hostile; on the contrary, like different sexes, they are complementary. They are the sugars and acids of fruit juices, the sugars being very much the same in all fruits, as regards their chemical composition, whilst the acids vary greatly according to the species of fruits, the nature of the soil in which they are grown, and their degree of ripeness when picked.

In the making of soft drinks, the sugars of fruit juice are replaced by what the makers call "syrup," "a solution of cane or beet sugar (cane for preference) in water so adjusted in proportions as to yield a uniform product of constant density and possessing an unvarying degree of sweetness." Saccharin, the sweetening power of which is so much greater than that of sugar—$\frac{1}{2}$ oz. saccharin equals $15\frac{1}{2}$ lb. sugar—is used in place of sugar by some makers, but it has a metallic taste which is unacceptable to a trained palate, besides which, it has no nutritive value whatsoever, such as sugar and sugar-made syrups have.

As regards acids, the soft drinks manufacturer uses chiefly tartaric, citric and malic acids. They are the acids which in their natural form are present in grapes, lemons and apples respectively. But the soft drinks manufacturer has many other

* We are indebted for most of the information contained in this section to the *Manufacture of Aerated Beverages, Cordials, etc., Seventh Edition*, published by Messrs. Stevenson and Howell, Ltd.

acids at his command, and he needs them, since all the drinks which he makes with some syrup are liable to ferment, a danger which is avoided chiefly by the use of hydrochloric and sulphuric acids.

Next in important to syrup and acids, there are the essences and colours upon which soft drinks depend for their individuality of flavour and appearance. Essences are the jealously guarded secret of each manufacturer of soft drinks, but colouring materials are offered for sale to all comers without any questions being asked. There are two distinct types of colours used to give soft drinks all the colours of the rainbow : the vegetable colours, such as burnt sugar and mint, and aniline colours, which are mostly used, as they provide a far greater range of shades—and they never fade. Aniline colours are distilled from coal tar.

Soft drinks which are most popular in the British Isles, may be divided into the following categories:—

1. Mineral waters.
2. Ginger ale and ginger beer.
3. Lemonade and lime juice.
4. Fruit "wines."
5. Cordials.

1.—MINERAL WATERS

Soda Water

The true aerated alkaline water known by this name is, strictly speaking, a medicament of the antacid type. It is not a beverage, if by this word we mean a pleasant thirst-quenching drink. Each 10-oz. egg-shaped bottle should consist of from 5 to 15 grains of bicarbonate of soda, dissolved in half a pint of water, and highly charged with carbonic acid gas. Indeed, the British Pharmacopœia orders 30 grains per pint, but that is not at all palatable and only intended as a medicine. It is a valuable remedy for sourness of the stomach, etc., but should not be taken as a regular beverage. To meet the public taste, or for other reasons, manufacturers of soda water and potash water vary the quantities of alkaline bicarbonate, according to their individual judgement or fancy. (*Law's Grocers' Manual.*)

2.—GINGER ALE AND GINGER BEER

Ginger Ale.

One of the most popular forms of minerals. It is made with

a few drops of essence of ginger, or capsicum extract, and a few drops of colouring matter; also some sugar or glucose, put into a bottle, which is then filled up with carbonated water. Occasionally a little mucilaginous matter, variously known technically as Froth, Heading, etc., is added to give ginger ale a "better head," and the drinker thereof a greater thrill.

Ginger Beer.

An effervescing beverage made by fermenting ginger, cream of tartar and sugar with yeast and water, and bottling before the fermentation is completed. The carbonic acid generated within the fluid gives, after a few days or weeks, an aerated drink; but this variety of ginger beer is also an alcoholic drink, for the fermentation which is set up by the yeast in a part of the sugar gives rise to a little alcohol, as well as to carbonic acid. Two per cent of alcohol is the strict legal limit. (*Law's Grocers' Manual.*)

3.—ARTIFICIAL LEMONADES. LIME JUICE, ETC.

Lemonade.

This is a generic name for all manner of thirst-quenching long drinks which taste of lemon juice. The plainest form is made from the juice of a lemon, cold water and a little sugar, but sparkling water may be used and different kinds of syrups in place of sugar.

Lemon Squash.

A bottled composition sold for the making of lemonade quickly and cheaply. One formula for its making is : soluble essence of lemon, $1\frac{1}{4}$ oz.; citric acid, 2 oz.; freshly boiled water, 6 oz.; and syrup to make 40 fluid oz. Colour, if desired, with a little saffron. (*Law's Grocers' Manual.*)

4.—ARTIFICIAL NON-ALCOHOLIC FRUIT "WINES"

All the so-called Wines have a common base : water, syrup, and citric acid. As regards colour, they are either red or yellow, being coloured either with a "red wine" dye or burnt sugar, or a "liquid lemon" dye. Their taste depends upon the "essence" used in their manufacture, and they are sold under the names of essences reputed to give them a flavour which approximates the fruits or flowers bearing the corresponding names, such as

Blackberry, Black Currant, Cherry, Cowslip, Damson, Elder-berry, Orange, Pineapple, Raisin, Raspberry, Red Currant, Sarsaparilla and Strawberry wines.

5.—Non-alcoholic Cordials

A non-alcoholic "cordial" is as much a contradiction in terms as a non-alcoholic "wine," since a "cordial" should have some beneficial action, either stimulating or steadying, upon the heart, whereas non-alcoholic so-called "cordials" are merely flavoured syrups, excessively sweet non-alcoholic "wines" which are intended to be diluted with water before consumption. They average 4 lb. of sugar to the gallon. So sweet a mixture is far from stable, and the ever-present danger of some form of fermentation makes it necessary to use either sulphurous acid or benzoic acid as a preventative.

THE END

INDEX

A CATALOGUE OF SELECTED DOVER BOOKS
IN ALL FIELDS OF INTEREST

A CATALOGUE OF SELECTED DOVER BOOKS IN ALL FIELDS OF INTEREST

AMERICA'S OLD MASTERS, James T. Flexner. Four men emerged unexpectedly from provincial 18th century America to leadership in European art: Benjamin West, J. S. Copley, C. R. Peale, Gilbert Stuart. Brilliant coverage of lives and contributions. Revised, 1967 edition. 69 plates. 365pp. of text.
21806-6 Paperbound $3.00

FIRST FLOWERS OF OUR WILDERNESS: AMERICAN PAINTING, THE COLONIAL PERIOD, James T. Flexner. Painters, and regional painting traditions from earliest Colonial times up to the emergence of Copley, West and Peale Sr., Foster, Gustavus Hesselius, Feke, John Smibert and many anonymous painters in the primitive manner. Engaging presentation, with 162 illustrations. xxii + 368pp.
22180-6 Paperbound $3.50

THE LIGHT OF DISTANT SKIES: AMERICAN PAINTING, 1760-1835, James T. Flexner. The great generation of early American painters goes to Europe to learn and to teach: West, Copley, Gilbert Stuart and others. Allston, Trumbull, Morse; also contemporary American painters—primitives, derivatives, academics—who remained in America. 102 illustrations. xiii + 306pp. 22179-2 Paperbound $3.00

A HISTORY OF THE RISE AND PROGRESS OF THE ARTS OF DESIGN IN THE UNITED STATES, William Dunlap. Much the richest mine of information on early American painters, sculptors, architects, engravers, miniaturists, etc. The only source of information for scores of artists, the major primary source for many others. Unabridged reprint of rare original 1834 edition, with new introduction by James T. Flexner, and 394 new illustrations. Edited by Rita Weiss. 6⅝ x 9⅝.
21695-0, 21696-9, 21697-7 Three volumes, Paperbound $13.50

EPOCHS OF CHINESE AND JAPANESE ART, Ernest F. Fenollosa. From primitive Chinese art to the 20th century, thorough history, explanation of every important art period and form, including Japanese woodcuts; main stress on China and Japan, but Tibet, Korea also included. Still unexcelled for its detailed, rich coverage of cultural background, aesthetic elements, diffusion studies, particularly of the historical period. 2nd, 1913 edition. 242 illustrations. lii + 439pp. of text.
20364-6, 20365-4 Two volumes, Paperbound $6.00

THE GENTLE ART OF MAKING ENEMIES, James A. M. Whistler. Greatest wit of his day deflates Oscar Wilde, Ruskin, Swinburne; strikes back at inane critics, exhibitions, art journalism; aesthetics of impressionist revolution in most striking form. Highly readable classic by great painter. Reproduction of edition designed by Whistler. Introduction by Alfred Werner. xxxvi + 334pp.
21875-9 Paperbound $2.50

ALPHABETS AND ORNAMENTS, Ernst Lehner. Well-known pictorial source for decorative alphabets, script examples, cartouches, frames, decorative title pages, calligraphic initials, borders, similar material. 14th to 19th century, mostly European. Useful in almost any graphic arts designing, varied styles. 750 illustrations. 256pp. 7 x 10. 21905-4 Paperbound $4.00

PAINTING: A CREATIVE APPROACH, Norman Colquhoun. For the beginner simple guide provides an instructive approach to painting: major stumbling blocks for beginner; overcoming them, technical points; paints and pigments; oil painting; watercolor and other media and color. New section on "plastic" paints. Glossary. Formerly *Paint Your Own Pictures.* 221pp. 22000-1 Paperbound $1.75

THE ENJOYMENT AND USE OF COLOR, Walter Sargent. Explanation of the relations between colors themselves and between colors in nature and art, including hundreds of little-known facts about color values, intensities, effects of high and low illumination, complementary colors. Many practical hints for painters, references to great masters. 7 color plates, 29 illustrations. x + 274pp.
20944-X Paperbound $2.50

THE NOTEBOOKS OF LEONARDO DA VINCI, compiled and edited by Jean Paul Richter. 1566 extracts from original manuscripts reveal the full range of Leonardo's versatile genius: all his writings on painting, sculpture, architecture, anatomy, astronomy, geography, topography, physiology, mining, music, etc., in both Italian and English, with 186 plates of manuscript pages and more than 500 additional drawings. Includes studies for the Last Supper, the lost Sforza monument, and other works. Total of xlvii + 866pp. 7⅞ x 10¾.
22572-0, 22573-9 Two volumes, Paperbound $10.00

MONTGOMERY WARD CATALOGUE OF 1895. Tea gowns, yards of flannel and pillow-case lace, stereoscopes, books of gospel hymns, the New Improved Singer Sewing Machine, side saddles, milk skimmers, straight-edged razors, high-button shoes, spittoons, and on and on . . . listing some 25,000 items, practically all illustrated. Essential to the shoppers of the 1890's, it is our truest record of the spirit of the period. Unaltered reprint of Issue No. 57, Spring and Summer 1895. Introduction by Boris Emmet. Innumerable illustrations. xiii + 624pp. 8½ x 11⅝.
22377-9 Paperbound $6.95

THE CRYSTAL PALACE EXHIBITION ILLUSTRATED CATALOGUE (LONDON, 1851). One of the wonders of the modern world—the Crystal Palace Exhibition in which all the nations of the civilized world exhibited their achievements in the arts and sciences—presented in an equally important illustrated catalogue. More than 1700 items pictured with accompanying text—ceramics, textiles, cast-iron work, carpets, pianos, sleds, razors, wall-papers, billiard tables, beehives, silverware and hundreds of other artifacts—represent the focal point of Victorian culture in the Western World. Probably the largest collection of Victorian decorative art ever assembled—indispensable for antiquarians and designers. Unabridged republication of the Art-Journal Catalogue of the Great Exhibition of 1851, with all terminal essays. New introduction by John Gloag, F.S.A. xxxiv + 426pp. 9 x 12.
22503-8 Paperbound $4.50

THE ARCHITECTURE OF COUNTRY HOUSES, Andrew J. Downing. Together with Vaux's *Villas and Cottages* this is the basic book for Hudson River Gothic architecture of the middle Victorian period. Full, sound discussions of general aspects of housing, architecture, style, decoration, furnishing, together with scores of detailed house plans, illustrations of specific buildings, accompanied by full text. Perhaps the most influential single American architectural book. 1850 edition. Introduction by J. Stewart Johnson. 321 figures, 34 architectural designs. xvi + 560pp.

22003-6 Paperbound $4.00

LOST EXAMPLES OF COLONIAL ARCHITECTURE, John Mead Howells. Full-page photographs of buildings that have disappeared or been so altered as to be denatured, including many designed by major early American architects. 245 plates. xvii + 248pp. 7⅞ x 10¾. 21143-6 Paperbound $3.00

DOMESTIC ARCHITECTURE OF THE AMERICAN COLONIES AND OF THE EARLY REPUBLIC, Fiske Kimball. Foremost architect and restorer of Williamsburg and Monticello covers nearly 200 homes between 1620-1825. Architectural details, construction, style features, special fixtures, floor plans, etc. Generally considered finest work in its area. 219 illustrations of houses, doorways, windows, capital mantels. xx + 314pp. 7⅞ x 10¾. 21743-4 Paperbound $3.50

EARLY AMERICAN ROOMS: 1650-1858, edited by Russell Hawes Kettell. Tour of 12 rooms, each representative of a different era in American history and each furnished, decorated, designed and occupied in the style of the era. 72 plans and elevations, 8-page color section, etc., show fabrics, wall papers, arrangements, etc. Full descriptive text. xvii + 200pp. of text. 8⅜ x 11¼.

21633-0 Paperbound $5.00

THE FITZWILLIAM VIRGINAL BOOK, edited by J. Fuller Maitland and W. B. Squire. Full modern printing of famous early 17th-century ms. volume of 300 works by Morley, Byrd, Bull, Gibbons, etc. For piano or other modern keyboard instrument; easy to read format. xxxvi + 938pp. 8⅜ x 11.

21068-5, 21069-3 Two volumes, Paperbound $8.00

HARPSICHORD MUSIC, Johann Sebastian Bach. Bach Gesellschaft edition. A rich selection of Bach's masterpieces for the harpsichord: the six English Suites, six French Suites, the six Partitas (Clavierübung part I), the Goldberg Variations (Clavierübung part IV), the fifteen Two-Part Inventions and the fifteen Three-Part Sinfonias. Clearly reproduced on large sheets with ample margins; eminently playable. vi + 312pp. 8⅛ x 11. 22360-4 Paperbound $5.00

THE MUSIC OF BACH: AN INTRODUCTION, Charles Sanford Terry. A fine, nontechnical introduction to Bach's music, both instrumental and vocal. Covers organ music, chamber music, passion music, other types. Analyzes themes, developments, innovations. x + 114pp. 21075-8 Paperbound $1.25

BEETHOVEN AND HIS NINE SYMPHONIES, Sir George Grove. Noted British musicologist provides best history, analysis, commentary on symphonies. Very thorough, rigorously accurate; necessary to both advanced student and amateur music lover. 436 musical passages. vii + 407 pp. 20334-4 Paperbound $2.25

JOHANN SEBASTIAN BACH, Philipp Spitta. One of the great classics of musicology, this definitive analysis of Bach's music (and life) has never been surpassed. Lucid, nontechnical analyses of hundreds of pieces (30 pages devoted to St. Matthew Passion, 26 to B Minor Mass). Also includes major analysis of 18th-century music. 450 musical examples. 40-page musical supplement. Total of xx + 1799pp.
(EUK) 22278-0, 22279-9 Two volumes, Clothbound $15.00

MOZART AND HIS PIANO CONCERTOS, Cuthbert Girdlestone. The only full-length study of an important area of Mozart's creativity. Provides detailed analyses of all 23 concertos, traces inspirational sources. 417 musical examples. Second edition. 509pp.　　　　　　　　　　　　　　　　(USO) 21271-8 Paperbound $3.50

THE PERFECT WAGNERITE: A COMMENTARY ON THE NIBLUNG'S RING, George Bernard Shaw. Brilliant and still relevant criticism in remarkable essays on Wagner's Ring cycle, Shaw's ideas on political and social ideology behind the plots, role of Leitmotifs, vocal requisites, etc. Prefaces. xxi + 136pp.
21707-8 Paperbound $1.50

DON GIOVANNI, W. A. Mozart. Complete libretto, modern English translation; biographies of composer and librettist; accounts of early performances and critical reaction. Lavishly illustrated. All the material you need to understand and appreciate this great work. Dover Opera Guide and Libretto Series; translated and introduced by Ellen Bleiler. 92 illustrations. 209pp.
21134-7 Paperbound $1.50

HIGH FIDELITY SYSTEMS: A LAYMAN'S GUIDE, Roy F. Allison. All the basic information you need for setting up your own audio system: high fidelity and stereo record players, tape records, F.M. Connections, adjusting tone arm, cartridge, checking needle alignment, positioning speakers, phasing speakers, adjusting hums, trouble-shooting, maintenance, and similar topics. Enlarged 1965 edition. More than 50 charts, diagrams, photos. iv + 91pp.　　　21514-8 Paperbound $1.25

REPRODUCTION OF SOUND, Edgar Villchur. Thorough coverage for laymen of high fidelity systems, reproducing systems in general, needles, amplifiers, preamps, loudspeakers, feedback, explaining physical background. "A rare talent for making technicalities vividly comprehensible," R. Darrell, High Fidelity. 69 figures. iv + 92pp.　　　　　　　　　　　　　　　　21515-6 Paperbound $1.00

HEAR ME TALKIN' TO YA: THE STORY OF JAZZ AS TOLD BY THE MEN WHO MADE IT, Nat Shapiro and Nat Hentoff. Louis Armstrong, Fats Waller, Jo Jones, Clarence Williams, Billy Holiday, Duke Ellington, Jelly Roll Morton and dozens of other jazz greats tell how it was in Chicago's South Side, New Orleans, depression Harlem and the modern West Coast as jazz was born and grew. xvi + 429pp.
21726-4 Paperbound $2.50

FABLES OF AESOP, translated by Sir Roger L'Estrange. A reproduction of the very rare 1931 Paris edition; a selection of the most interesting fables, together with 50 imaginative drawings by Alexander Calder. v + 128pp. 6½x9¼.
21780-9 Paperbound $1.25

TWO LITTLE SAVAGES; BEING THE ADVENTURES OF TWO BOYS WHO LIVED AS INDIANS AND WHAT THEY LEARNED, Ernest Thompson Seton. Great classic of nature and boyhood provides a vast range of woodlore in most palatable form, a genuinely entertaining story. Two farm boys build a teepee in woods and live in it for a month, working out Indian solutions to living problems, star lore, birds and animals, plants, etc. 293 illustrations. vii + 286pp.

20985-7 Paperbound $2.50

PETER PIPER'S PRACTICAL PRINCIPLES OF PLAIN & PERFECT PRONUNCIATION. Alliterative jingles and tongue-twisters of surprising charm, that made their first appearance in America about 1830. Republished in full with the spirited woodcut illustrations from this earliest American edition. 32pp. $4\frac{1}{2}$ x $6\frac{3}{8}$.

22560-7 Paperbound $1.00

SCIENCE EXPERIMENTS AND AMUSEMENTS FOR CHILDREN, Charles Vivian. 73 easy experiments, requiring only materials found at home or easily available, such as candles, coins, steel wool, etc.; illustrate basic phenomena like vacuum, simple chemical reaction, etc. All safe. Modern, well-planned. Formerly *Science Games for Children*. 102 photos, numerous drawings. 96pp. $6\frac{1}{8}$ x $9\frac{1}{4}$.

21856-2 Paperbound $1.25

AN INTRODUCTION TO CHESS MOVES AND TACTICS SIMPLY EXPLAINED, Leonard Barden. Informal intermediate introduction, quite strong in explaining reasons for moves. Covers basic material, tactics, important openings, traps, positional play in middle game, end game. Attempts to isolate patterns and recurrent configurations. Formerly *Chess*. 58 figures. 102pp. (USO) 21210-6 Paperbound $1.25

LASKER'S MANUAL OF CHESS, Dr. Emanuel Lasker. Lasker was not only one of the five great World Champions, he was also one of the ablest expositors, theorists, and analysts. In many ways, his Manual, permeated with his philosophy of battle, filled with keen insights, is one of the greatest works ever written on chess. Filled with analyzed games by the great players. A single-volume library that will profit almost any chess player, beginner or master. 308 diagrams. xli x 349pp.

20640-8 Paperbound $2.75

THE MASTER BOOK OF MATHEMATICAL RECREATIONS, Fred Schuh. In opinion of many the finest work ever prepared on mathematical puzzles, stunts, recreations; exhaustively thorough explanations of mathematics involved, analysis of effects, citation of puzzles and games. Mathematics involved is elementary. Translated by F. Göbel. 194 figures. xxiv + 430pp.

22134-2 Paperbound $3.00

MATHEMATICS, MAGIC AND MYSTERY, Martin Gardner. Puzzle editor for Scientific American explains mathematics behind various mystifying tricks: card tricks, stage "mind reading," coin and match tricks, counting out games, geometric dissections, etc. Probability sets, theory of numbers clearly explained. Also provides more than 400 tricks, guaranteed to work, that you can do. 135 illustrations. xii + 176pp.

20338-2 Paperbound $1.50

MATHEMATICAL PUZZLES FOR BEGINNERS AND ENTHUSIASTS, Geoffrey Mott-Smith. 189 puzzles from easy to difficult—involving arithmetic, logic, algebra, properties of digits, probability, etc.—for enjoyment and mental stimulus. Explanation of mathematical principles behind the puzzles. 135 illustrations. viii + 248pp.

20198-8 Paperbound $1.25

PAPER FOLDING FOR BEGINNERS, William D. Murray and Francis J. Rigney. Easiest book on the market, clearest instructions on making interesting, beautiful origami. Sail boats, cups, roosters, frogs that move legs, bonbon boxes, standing birds, etc. 40 projects; more than 275 diagrams and photographs. 94pp.

20713-7 Paperbound $1.00

TRICKS AND GAMES ON THE POOL TABLE, Fred Herrmann. 79 tricks and games—some solitaires, some for two or more players, some competitive games—to entertain you between formal games. Mystifying shots and throws, unusual caroms, tricks involving such props as cork, coins, a hat, etc. Formerly *Fun on the Pool Table*. 77 figures. 95pp.

21814-7 Paperbound $1.00

HAND SHADOWS TO BE THROWN UPON THE WALL: A SERIES OF NOVEL AND AMUSING FIGURES FORMED BY THE HAND, Henry Bursill. Delightful picturebook from great-grandfather's day shows how to make 18 different hand shadows: a bird that flies, duck that quacks, dog that wags his tail, camel, goose, deer, boy, turtle, etc. Only book of its sort. vi + 33pp. 6½ x 9¼. 21779-5 Paperbound $1.00

WHITTLING AND WOODCARVING, E. J. Tangerman. 18th printing of best book on market. "If you can cut a potato you can carve" toys and puzzles, chains, chessmen, caricatures, masks, frames, woodcut blocks, surface patterns, much more. Information on tools, woods, techniques. Also goes into serious wood sculpture from Middle Ages to present, East and West. 464 photos, figures. x + 293pp.

20965-2 Paperbound $2.00

HISTORY OF PHILOSOPHY, Julián Marias. Possibly the clearest, most easily followed, best planned, most useful one-volume history of philosophy on the market; neither skimpy nor overfull. Full details on system of every major philosopher and dozens of less important thinkers from pre-Socratics up to Existentialism and later. Strong on many European figures usually omitted. Has gone through dozens of editions in Europe. 1966 edition, translated by Stanley Appelbaum and Clarence Strowbridge. xviii + 505pp. 21739-6 Paperbound $3.00

YOGA: A SCIENTIFIC EVALUATION, Kovoor T. Behanan. Scientific but non-technical study of physiological results of yoga exercises; done under auspices of Yale U. Relations to Indian thought, to psychoanalysis, etc. 16 photos. xxiii + 270pp.

20505-3 Paperbound $2.50